COLLECTING GOLD DUST

Nurturing the Dhamma in Daily Living

Sayadaw U Tejaniya

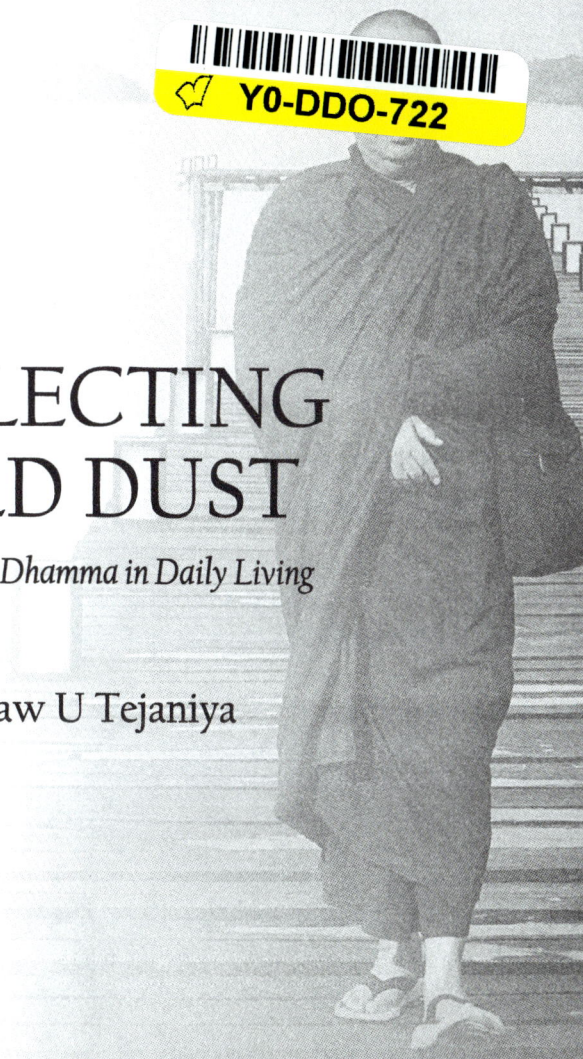

COLLECTING GOLD DUST
Nurturing the Dhamma in Daily Living

Sayadaw U Tejaniya

Transcribed by Tony Reardon
Edited by Laura Zan

Collecting Gold Dust: Nurturing the Dhamma in Daily Living
Copyright © Sayadaw U Tejaniya 2019
Transcribed by *Tony Reardon* and edited by *Laura Zan*

Shwe Oo Min Dhamma Sukha Tawya Meditation Center
Aung Myay Thar Yar Street, Kon Tala Paung Village, Mingaladon Township, PO 11022 Yangon, Myanmar

For Dhamma materials, please visit: www.ashintejaniya.org

Publisher's Cataloging-in-Publication data
    Names: Tejaniya, Sayadaw U., author.
    Title: Collecting gold dust: nurturing the Dhamma in daily living / Sayadaw U Tejaniya.
    Description: Berkeley [California] : Wisdom Streams Foundation, 2019. Paperback. Appendix included.
    Identifiers: ISBN: 978-0-9835844-5-2
    Subjects: LCSH: Meditation. | Mindfulness. | Satipaṭṭhāna (Buddhism). | Theravāda Buddhism.
    BISAC: BODY, MIND & SPIRIT / Mindfulness & Meditation.
    Classification: LCC BQ5630.S2 | DDC 294.3–dc22

First Printing 3,000 copies, June 2019 by Wisdom Streams Foundation in North America
Published with permission for free distribution by Wisdom Streams Foundation (North America)
To request books or to support future printing of Dhamma books for free distribution, please go to:
www.wisdomstreams.org | info@wisdomstreams.org

Published in Asia by Auspicious Affinity with permission for free distribution
First Printing 5,000 copies, June 2019
Auspicious Affinity
P.O.Box 08738, Pejabat Pos Kelana Jaya, 46796 Petaling Jaya, Selangor, MALAYSIA
Email: auspiciousaffinity@gmail.com

Cover design, layout & photography by *Hor Tuck Loon* assisted by *Chan Lai Fun*
Front cover image purchased from *iStock by Getty Images* (Order No. 2059259629)
Printed by *Percetakan Osacar Sdn Bhd*, Malaysia

Books in print for free distribution:
Don't Look Down on the Defilements: They will Laugh at You (2006), Awareness Alone is not Enough (2008),
Dhamma Everywhere: Welcoming Each Moment with Awareness + Wisdom (2011)

Shambhala publication:
When Awareness Becomes Natural: A Guide to Cultivating Mindfulness in Everyday Life (2016)

Namo Tassa Bhagavato Arahato Sammā-Sambuddhassa

Homage to Him, the Blessed One, the Worthy One,
the Perfectly Self-Enlightened One

You have to play,
play with awareness
and the mind.
Then it becomes very interesting.
Use your know-how and wit.
If meditation feels like a responsibility,
it'll just be a burden.
Create your world.
*It's a game called **Master Mind**.*

Acknowledgements

My special gratitude goes to my teacher, the late Venerable Shwe Oo Min Sayadaw Bhaddanta Kosalla Mahāthera, who taught me the Dhamma and right attitude for my spiritual development and meditation practice.

I want to express my appreciation to all yogis. Their questions and difficulties have once again inspired many of the explanations in this book. I really hope that this book will help yogis better understand mindfulness meditation and deepen their practice.

Finally, I would like to thank everyone who has contributed to the completion of this book.

Sayadaw U Tejaniya

Dear Reader

It doesn't take long for a yogi (meditator) new to Sayadaw U Tejaniya to notice humor permeating his teachings. Whether it is making an observation on his surroundings or commenting on the environment of the mind, Sayadaw, or "the Teacher" as his disciples fondly call him, delivers his teachings with a good dose of wit.

While the delivery may come with a bit of levity, Sayadaw is quite serious about the subject of Dhamma. Using his own experiences as guide and gradually honing his presentation, Sayadaw encourages meditators to always be persistent, experiment, and dig deeper into the Dhamma. He relates to his lay students through pithy business metaphors and regularly describes his own experiences in learning to meditate in the midst of managing the family business and before ordaining permanently in 1996.

Sayadaw is a strong proponent of applying the Buddha's teachings to daily activities in a monastery, at home, and at work. When his long-time disciples make the migration to the Shwe Oo Min Dhamma Sukha

Tawya Meditation Center in Yangon, Myanmar, one of his first questions is typically about their practice. Some may reply in detail while others sheepishly answer that they have returned to jumpstart their flagging practice.

Sayadaw often encourages yogis to continue cultivating their own energy and wisdom after a retreat. To help post-retreat, some of Sayadaw's retreats even have participants going mindfully about their business during the day in their own homes or workplaces and discussing their experiences and discoveries in evening and weekend Q&A sessions. Other retreats have incorporated mindful talking periods during the day.

Meditating in daily life means building up these skills with diligence and right inquiry. It means asking the right questions at the right time to spur on an internal curiosity to investigate further. The answers will reveal themselves to appropriate questions so long as we apply right view and perseverance to our meditation, Sayadaw reassures us. When meditation gathers momentum, awareness becomes more natural. There is less doing and more recognizing.

This book was compiled as a continuing thread to the question of *what next*? We each have our own versions of the first few days of retreat excitement calming down to a steady mind, building momentum over a week or two, only to see it crumble in the anticipation of reentering daily life. *Forgetfulness* sets in as we leave Sayadaw's presence and the supportive environment of the center. Even in the occasional outing to the village or city while at the Shwe Oo Min Meditation Center, yogis often report to Sayadaw that *there are just so many objects out there!* To which Sayadaw often replies that there are only six sense doors and knowing is of only the six senses at the six sense doors inside and out of retreat. Sayadaw noted in a recent retreat in California that most of us meet a limited set of people in our daily lives and go about our lives with a limited set of people, pointing out that if we observed our reactions to others with right view, we could learn to resolve these challenges ourselves. Mostly we don't watch and often not with right view.

It is our hope that Sayadaw's words will inspire all of us to continue wholeheartedly, being as sincere and serious as Sayadaw is about being aware and cultivating awareness at home. In compiling these pages, we asked ourselves: What are the most salient issues to practicing in daily life? What might arise more off the cushion that we may not experience as much on retreat? What stories from Sayadaw's own experiences can address the challenges of daily life practice? To get at some of these answers, we have tracked down and edited transcriptions from the more recent retreats abroad. While Sayadaw teaches through guided meditations and Q&As led by yogi questions, we have compiled this book thematically so that a reader can use it in daily life.

What do we do when the retreat is over? "Mindfulness is a Lifestyle Change" begins the book while an abbreviated "Mindfulness in Brief" caps the book in Appendix. The beginning chapters address the triumvirate of greed, aversion, and delusion while latter chapters delve into more specific topics for daily life, which is anytime, anywhere off the cushion although we could also be practicing on the cushion in our daily lives as well! While it may seem at odds to have sections on cultivating wholesome minds, inquiry, and non-doing all in the same book, each of these pieces answers different needs at different times in our meditation practice, whether within a span of minutes or months.

It feels like we have been editing for quite some time, and we have, over some years, having worked on this manuscript in the midst of daily life, and understand fully when life just takes over. We have tried to stick to our own page limits for this daily-life book, lest we continue to edit forever! If this is the first book you are picking up with Sayadaw U Tejaniya's teachings, may we suggest the illustrated *Don't Look Down on the Defilements* for a funny and quick primer on the right attitude for meditation, *Dhamma Everywhere: Welcoming Each Moment with Awareness + Wisdom* for a more in-depth look, and *Awareness Alone is Not Enough* with Q&A's from different retreats? These are all given out freely and can be accessed online at www.ashintejaniya.org or through Wisdom Streams, www.wisdomstreams.org in North America. For more auditory learners, please check for Sayadaw's retreat audio on www.dharmaseed.org. *When Awareness Becomes Natural: A Guide to Cultivating Mindfulness in Everyday Life* is a commercial publication that can be accessed through Shambhala and other sources. We appreciate greatly your very vital contributions towards future free publications globally; please reach out to any of us at info@wisdomstreams.org.

When we welcome the Dhamma into our daily lives we reap the benefits of the Buddha's teachings. Our deepest gratitude goes to Sayadaw for patiently lighting this path of *awareness + wisdom,* and teaching us the right attitude for meditation. May all living beings benefit from the dedication of those who have contributed to this process: Ma Thet (Moushumi Ghosh) for her tireless and dedicated retreat translations which are in this book, and for her careful telling of Sayadaw's story in "A Note from the Teacher," to all the folks who sent in transcriptions and those who did not shy away from our drafts in their roughest states. A big thank you to Sheng Bin Chiu, Sajama Sajama, TJ, Jim Noyes, Tom Aust, Ashin Sunanda, Steve Armstrong, Douglas McGill, Martin Kaminer, Nancy Zan, Margaret Smith, Heidi Che, Chan Lai Fun, Tiffany Taalman, and Jie Zeng for joining us at different stages with your patient and close reading of the material. We have immense gratitude to folks globally who will be bringing this book to life with dana, layout, printing, and distribution including Chan Lai Fun and Hor Tuck Loon.

May the reader benefit from this project as much as we have collaborating on it. We assume responsibility for any errors in the transcription or editing and will do our best to rectify any issues for future editions. Do email comments to info@wisdomstreams.org attention Laura.

Finally, this book is by no means comprehensive, and not meant to replace Sayadaw's personal guidance or your own further exploration of the Dhamma. Good luck in your endeavors!

This book is dedicated to all the beings in the universe. ☺

With much mettā,
Tony Reardon
Laura Zan

On Language

We work within the limits of language to describe the process of clear seeing that is at times difficult to pin down with words. As such, some rules of grammar may be bent a teeny bit. A construct like "the mind is knowing" instead of "the mind knows" is used in instances where it seems more appropriate to describe something in process. The following words are used interchangeably: *watching, being aware, observing, being mindful, recognizing, noticing, and paying attention.* You may also see the word "yogi" used often, which is Sayadaw's reference to a meditator. "Dhamma" with a big "D" refers to the teachings of the Buddha and the practice of meditation while "dhamma" with a little "d" refers to natural phenomena, natural law, or object.

We have tried to maintain Sayadaw's voice as much as possible throughout. The combination word "awareness + wisdom," first coined by Sayadaw, but used freely before the book *Dhamma Everywhere* came out, underscores the need for more than mere awareness in vipassanā (insight) meditation. Sayadaw always maintained that his teacher, the late Shwe Oo Min Sayadaw, referred to awareness with the assumption of inherent wisdom.

We have also used the singular "they" as a gender-neutral pronoun where possible.

Pāḷi and English words have been used throughout the book although we have limited Pāḷi usage to make this daily life book as accessible as possible.

Contents

A Note from the Teacher

You may be finished with a formal retreat for now but remember that the dhamma is everything, so it is everywhere, all the time. Don't lose track of that. You can persevere and continue practicing at home. Practicing the Dhamma includes all the practices of right thought (which is a fundamental part of right view), right speech, and right action. Practicing the Dhamma begins with a mindset change that, if we are able to take it on, may eventually lead to a lifestyle change. It is really worth the effort. The right efforts bear fruit when sufficient conditions are fulfilled. The Buddha said, "If you look after the Dhamma, the Dhamma will look after you." Looking after the Dhamma simply means practicing it. After a certain point, the Dhamma will carry you along on its wave. So keep going!

What is dhamma? It is everything: all of nature, its causes and effects; the mind that is meditating (i.e. the qualities of awareness, perseverance, stability of mind, faith, and wisdom); it is everything that becomes observed in meditation (the sensations, the six sense objects which include the mind as a sense object, the experiences, the events, the thoughts, the pleasant, unpleasant, and neutral feelings) and also that which we may or may not consciously notice yet. These are all a part of our experience. By meditating, we are growing the qualities of awareness, perseverance, stability of mind, faith, and wisdom.

These qualities when strong are called powers (bala) and they protect us, look after us, and bring us good results. So long as we are practicing, we are using the qualities of awareness (remembering what is wholesome), perseverance, wisdom, faith, and stability of mind. Over many years of retreats with my teacher, the late Shwe Oo Min Sayadaw ("Sayadawgyi"), I developed these powers, yet I did not use them in life and did not practice them except on retreat. I had to truly dedicate myself to them before I understood what "Dhammaṃ saraṇaṃ gacchāmi: I go to the Dhamma for refuge" truly meant and what a true refuge the Dhamma truly is.

I was about 13 years old when I started to meditate. I worked with a technique that required energetic, rhythmic breathing and got hooked on the pleasant physical sensation and calm that the experience brought. When I told Sayadawgyi about this and that I liked it, he was curious and asked me about my experiences. He would tell me stories of other people's special meditation experiences and this would make me want such experiences and motivated me to meditate very diligently. I quickly caught on that when I maintained detailed mindfulness throughout the day, the feelings of calm and pleasantness could be sustained so I was zealous in maintaining mindfulness. He also told me something that really stuck with me: be happy when I noticed anything about myself because it meant that I was aware of myself, that I was mindful. I was so focused on the mindfulness that anything I noticed about myself became a source of joy: it meant I was mindful! It never mattered to me even if I discovered an undesirable quality because the point I saw was that I was mindful.

Sayadawgyi often asked me *why* certain things happened when I went to him to describe my experiences. One episode in particular was when he asked me to find out why the abdomen rises and falls (that was my main object at that time) and I said it was because of the breath. Then he asked why there was breathing. I did not know this answer, which prompted a six-day search to find out. Every day, at every sit, the question dogged my observation of the breath and I remember on day six when the curious mind thought about why it was breathing and I saw the desire to breathe. This episode and the success I had in finding the answer was so thrilling that I ran out of the dhamma hall immediately to tell my teacher the

Wisdom is one word but it encompasses so much and operates in many ways.

answer. It has fueled an eternal curiosity in me to observe and investigate, which of course has led to all sorts of discoveries.

Many types of insights can be awakened. Insights into the nature of things include insights into the nature of our own practice, insights into the nature of awareness, insights into the nature of the things we observe and experience, insights into the nature of things as they are and more. Although we may not always realize it, just persevering and noticing is the main skill we need. Whenever awareness is established and strong, and we have an insight, we will begin to see nature in ways that we had never conceived of before and see things in ways we had never seen before. This is the growth of wisdom. Our work and our practice is always changing with this wisdom.

Wisdom is one word but it encompasses so much and operates in many ways. Sometimes we miss the fact that it is there and doing its work because we are not familiar with the nature of wisdom and its various job descriptions. We are more familiar with *making an effort*, like yogis making a physical effort not to be sleepy. Instead, when we are sleepy we could actually check out the sleepiness, if we are curious, and wisdom would at once be at work: *Why is there sleepiness now? What has brought it on? What does it feel like?* What we mostly do instead is resist this state because of our belief that sleepiness is not good when we are meditating. We react negatively as a result and try to do something immediately to fix the experience rather than seeing it as it is and checking it out. I recall my teacher's first lesson to me: when I notice anything about myself, it means there is awareness. That is a good thing.

I also had a first taste of the importance of the mind after an incident with a bed bug. I loved the feeling of calm that came with continuous mindfulness and the attendant samādhi (stability of mind) so much that I would forgo sleep to enjoy this bliss. One night a bed bug bit me while I was meditating in my room in the middle of the night. Even though this disrupted the blissful feelings, I was unperturbed. I knew I could get it back so I continued meditating but it didn't come back. I tried harder, I walked, I sat, and I still did not sleep. I became obsessed with regaining the blissful feeling, to no avail. I continued to the morning, the whole day, the next night, the next day. By day three I had a headache but I didn't give up. I put medicated plasters that relieve muscle soreness at my temples and continued my efforts, until finally it got too much and too painful, that I gave up. I surrendered. Never mind if I couldn't have that bliss back, I thought. I just dropped it and continued to meditate without any more desire to achieve that bliss. It came back, just like that. As I simply paid attention to what I was doing, without a thought of having any more of the bliss, it was back. And I learned this huge lesson about meditation, which has stayed with me ever since, and I ran all the way to my teacher's kuti (cottage) to tell him and he hammered home the bitter lesson, saying, "Well if you can get it by doing it, then do it."

I didn't know the mind directly then, but I just realized very deeply that greed was neither useful nor helpful when practicing meditation. It had no place in getting me results. So I never had greed when I meditated anymore. Ironically that did not prevent me from having greed in many other aspects of my life, so much so that it led to depression.

When I was around 18 to 20 years old on one of my retreats with my teacher, I remember Sayadawgyi mentioning that we can ask what the mind is aware of. Until then, in all my retreats over the years, although I was totally dedicated to being mindful on retreat, I simply watched my body movements and sensations. When thoughts were noticed, I acknowledged them then returned to the task of being aware of all my bodily movements and sensations, over and over again all day long. I recalled my teacher's words the next morning as I was brushing my teeth and when I posed the question, it felt like a weight was suddenly taken off my mind. As it was, my practice had built up quite a bit of momentum on the retreat so when the attention turned to what the mind was aware of, and what the mind knew, there was suddenly so much to know! It took off! I saw the mind and whatever it knew. From then on, my practice changed. Whenever I went on retreat, I would, in sitting and in all activities, lead with the question: What is the mind knowing? What is the mind aware of? This opened up the practice immensely at the center.

At home, the practice was forgotten and I got busy having fun with my friends. At University to study engineering, I became so involved in having so much fun with my friends that I flunked my second year of Regional College. At about this time, my oldest brother passed away from leukemia at the age of 43, and my father needed help running his menswear shop in a bustling wholesale center in downtown Yangon, a walking distance from our home. My father decided to take me out of University, no doubt a fact that I was a non-doctor in a family filled with brothers and a sister studying medicine. The only other brother not studying medicine had already finished University and was helping my father with the shop.

I wanted so much to continue to be with my friends that I actually, while helping out at the shop, still tried to repeat my second year at

University on my own. It was not as much fun anymore by then because all my friends had already moved on to the main Rangoon University for their third year in Engineering studies while I was still at the Regional College. It was discouraging, so I stopped trying to repeat the year. I slowly descended into depression from resentment, fear, dissatisfaction, having to do what I did not want to, and not being able to do what I wanted to do. It was the love, or actually greed for fun that indirectly led to my years of depression.

Initially I forgot about my unhappiness after a while, because it wasn't very strong then and the depression seemed to go away. When it returned a second time, I got fed up of feeling mopey and angrily railed against the emotion and willed myself to overcome it that way.

While I was working with my father, I got more of an opportunity to go for longer retreats at my teacher's monastery too, than when I had been in school. My father had no objections to my going and I mostly did the customary days off during the Burmese New Year. At one point I thought I wanted to be a monk for life and told my family and my teacher and they were all happy for me. Ten months in, my mind had changed again, and I just could not stay at the center any longer. My teacher gently tried to persuade me to stay but when my mind was made

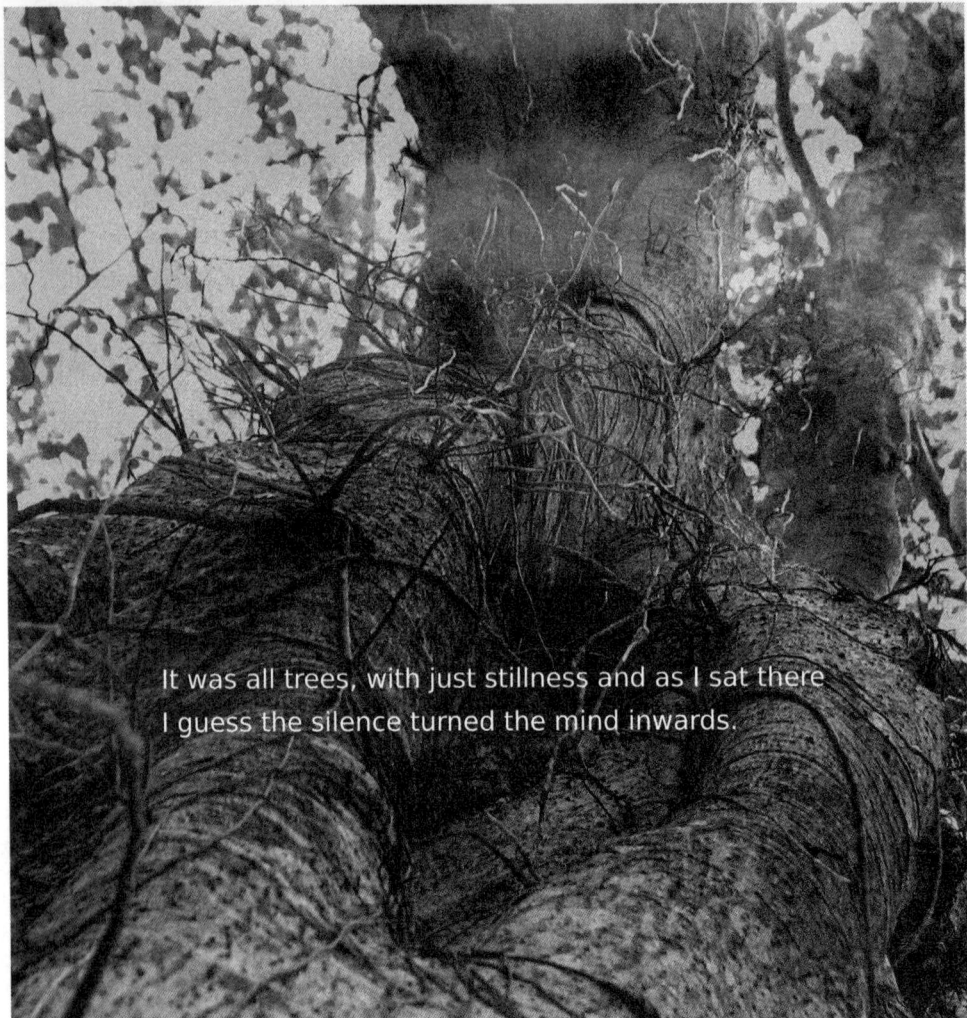

It was all trees, with just stillness and as I sat there
I guess the silence turned the mind inwards.

up there was no changing it. I went home. Ironically it was right on the way home in the taxi from that retreat that I actually descended into the deepest depression of my life. In hindsight, I think the feelings that came up had something to do with some insights into dukkha not being fully understood or realized. Sitting in the taxi on the way home I began to feel irrational fears. I was sure the policeman on the street knew about all my misbehaviors. I went home fearful. This time I could not shake the feelings that overtook me and it was two long years of depression at home before I finally turned in desperation to meditation again, but this time I did not go to the monastery. Circumstances did not permit. My father was getting older and I could not take time off like I had done before. I did try to take short holidays to places I had gone to with my friends before but nothing helped. I could not be happy. I only sought out meditation when it became my very last resort.

When I finally, in my exhausted and suffering mind, decided maybe I should try meditating at home, something I'd never done before then, I went to speak to my teacher. Sayadawgyi just told me to try. I accompanied my teacher for a four- to five-day retreat to a monastery about 10 miles out of Bago that he was visiting to give myself a boost. It was probably my time because I had three insights while meditating at that monastery that gave me some impetus to persevere when I went home. When I got to the monastery, I spent my time practicing as I already knew well how to. The second day, I sat under a tree because there was not much to do out there, except to watch. It was all trees, with just stillness and as I sat there I guess the silence turned the mind inwards. Suddenly, I saw all the rage, resentment, fear, desires, and frustrations that were racing through my mind. I was shocked. I saw it was all negative thinking in the mind. I realized if I died with the mind in this state, it was not going to a good state/place. That was the first thing that made me afraid to die, not in general, but right then in that state.

The next day as I was taking a shower at a well, pulling up one pail of water after another and pouring it over myself in the heat, a man came running down a hillside. He was large and very dark, his skin almost black, that he must have been in the heat a long time. He was sweating profusely and panting hard and he said to me as he ran towards me, "Water, water" and silently I handed him the pail full of water that I pulled up from the well. He turned the pail up to drink directly from it and drank till all the water was gone! Then he ran off. I just stared at him. Then it dawned on me after he left that I was all alone in that area. The monastery had a lot of land. My watch, which I had taken off, was on the edge of the well. I knew the area had prisons somewhere. And the appearance of the man was not ordinary. I got the chills. I could have been robbed and killed if he had had any ill intentions. Again, the thought came to me that I was not ready to die in my current state of mind.

Then the next night, in my last night with my teacher before I was going to battle it out on my own at home, he asked me to get him medicine from the dining cottage. The monks' kutis were far from each other and it was pitch dark but I knew the land well and there was moonlight so I walked without lighting the flashlight I had with me. As I walked back to my teacher's kuti at one point I just felt like using the flashlight so I flashed it and stopped dead. Right in front of me was a viper. One more step and my foot would have been struck. My blood ran cold, the hair on my head (although shaved bald) stood and all I could do was stand. I was so transfixed with fear that I could not move. The snake moved away by itself but I remained there, standing still until my teacher sent his attendant monk to come find me and I followed him back to my teacher's kuti. I really felt the fear of death then. I was really afraid that I might die.

Of course mindfulness was not continuous when I got home from that "kick-starter" retreat. I knew how to watch the mind, I knew about the watching mind or awareness of awareness and I could use the six sense objects just fine, and although I often speak to yogis about using questions, I myself initially had none. I was only meditating to calm the mind a little, as much as possible. Fear and anxiety overwhelmed me, and when the feelings were really strong, I would sometimes use the feeling as the object and watch them continuously until the feeling subsided. Other times, they wouldn't hold my attention long enough and I used my breath to anchor my mind. These objects of the feelings and the breath were familiar to me and I knew how to use these objects to anchor the mind. I did not begin using other objects until months afterwards. Without attention on an object, the fear and anxiety could quickly become scary, and, if they became overwhelming, I used the inhaler because the sharp menthol smell and the sensation in my sinuses and forehead would bring my attention to these sensations and off the thoughts that fueled the emotions.

The suffering feeling reminded me to be mindful and that mindfulness made me feel a bit better each time I was mindful. I visited my teacher every week or two and told him about my practice and complained about how hard it was to keep practicing at home. He would tell me it takes time to find our footing and encouraged me to keep trying. My problem was not one of ability to practice. It was more because the peace I got from meditation was not lasting. I already benefited from keeping up the mindfulness—it did give me relief from the suffering—but it did not give a lasting peace, which I craved. I didn't want to suffer and the temporary peace I got did not satisfy the mind's craving. It was demotivating yet I had to keep at it; otherwise, the mental suffering came back. This in hindsight was a blessing in disguise!

I worked at my father's shop, trying to cope with the demands of the business in my state of anxiety, uncertainty, and fear. I often felt unable to make the decisions that had to be made. Very often, the decisions just had to be made, without regard as to whether they were right or wrong, because my state of mind did not allow me this perspective. Sometimes I would make the wrong decisions and had to deal with the fall out of that too. Through it all, I would turn my attention to the suffering, or the breath as much as I could. If the feelings were particularly harsh, I could neither face those feelings nor watch the breath successfully, then I turned to the mentholated inhaler. The Vicks inhaler is a small tube with some mentholated ointment or oil inside that one can inhale through the tube. The sensation in the nose when I inhaled it would help to bring the mind's attention back, and if I was really desperate I would inhale sharply to get a really strong sharp sensation that would get the mind's attention, helping to gain control over getting mentally overwhelmed.

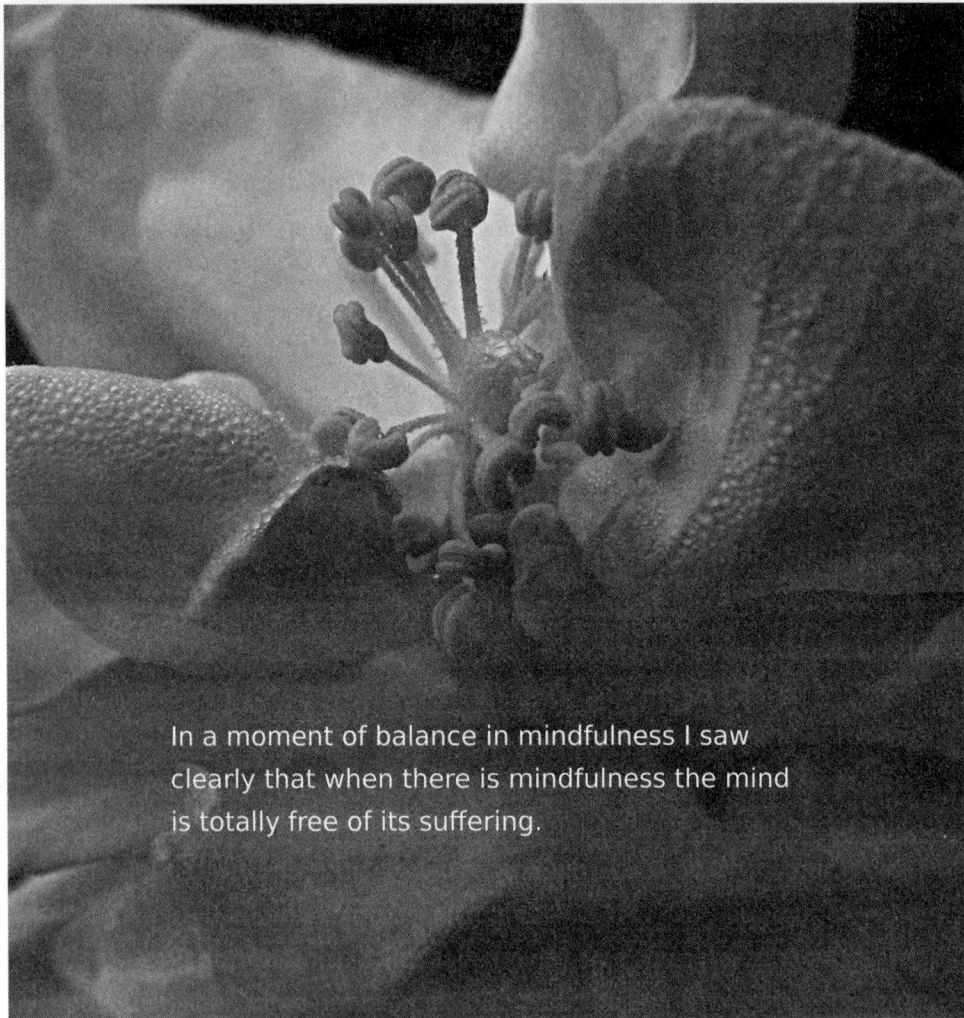

In a moment of balance in mindfulness I saw clearly that when there is mindfulness the mind is totally free of its suffering.

During these initial two months I also began reading the books of Mogok Sayadaw. I happened to see my friend with one of a series of 36 books on Mogok Sayadaw's teachings and eventually borrowed about six books over some months. Reading a few pages of these books every night, I eventually realized that Mogok Sayadaw was pointing to check to see how the mind is reacting to whatever it is knowing, over and over, constantly.

About two months after I began trying to practice at home and at work, the mind did begin to gain some balance. Where I could not previously think without the cloud and background of anxious fears and doubts, I now began to be able to consider things more rationally and logically. And one day I had a moment of clarity. In a moment of balance in mindfulness I saw clearly that when there is mindfulness the mind is totally free of its suffering. Then the suffering returned, but the insight had been strong. Although it was just a glimpse, the mind saw this truth unquestionably. There is a place of utter peace. And the conviction that it gave the mind provided me with the motivation to continue practicing with increased vigor. I knew now that this was the way out, for sure, so there was a real desire to practice. I began to think about practice daily, about how to practice.

After about six months practicing at home, the depression had gradually disappeared and I began to notice that I would notice my reactions whenever I looked at people or when I heard something. The thoughts and feelings had calmed down enough and the practice had gained enough momentum that I finally had the mental space and interest to use objects outside of the breath or feelings. The practice became interesting in and of itself, and I began initially just one at a time to explore the mind's ability to stay anchored, for example on one pair of fingertips touching while sitting in the shop, on myself when drinking coffee or tea during a break, or being aware of seeing while waiting for customers, and so on.

And these accumulated practices of collecting the mind enabled me to then be more aware of the interactions within my own mind when I was making decisions, counting money or attending to customers. I could notice when I lost my composure and devise a plan for maintaining it in my next interaction, always using the practice of collecting the mind as the basis for strengthening the mind's composure. As these interactions happened daily and routinely, this is how I learned what helped me to maintain the composure of my mind, what helped me to remain aware and maintain continuity—when I needed to pick up attention on one object, mainly when I was no longer interacting with someone else or doing a task and when I needed to be aware in a more fluid way as in when customers approached and I had to attend to them and interact with them. The awareness became closer to continuous and insights naturally arose more and more over time.

A year in, I read an article about the ājīvaṭṭhamaka sīla, eight precepts with right livelihood as the eighth precept. I was particularly interested in the expansion of the precept on not telling untruths, into four precepts for right speech: refraining from telling lies, slander, harsh speech, and idle chatter. I was inspired to try this. The depression had already made me quite subdued at the marketplace I worked at, compared to the joker I had been previously, and then practicing continuously made me quieter.

However, taking on the four right speech precepts left me with hardly anything to say because I now avoided idle chatter. If someone came over to gossip about some other stallholder, they no longer found in me someone that sympathized. I merely listened and did not contribute as I saw neither wisdom nor meaning in adding fuel to their fire. The mindfulness became so much keener, aware of everything I said or planned to say and naturally the strength and composure of the mind also improved.

After two years of practicing dedicatedly I began to notice that I had been avoiding unnecessary interactions and I began to challenge myself to go to social functions as a representative of my family and maintain mindfulness, or to go out for dinner with old friends and maintain my mindfulness, composure, or my stand without frustration or rudeness when they tried to get me to join them in drinking alcohol. I even went for a boxing match and learned a lasting lesson that this was not the place for me any longer.

I tell you this story to say this is possible for you as well. You just have to persevere, experiment, and use your wisdom to figure out what works until this also becomes a natural part of your life. I want to persuade you that this is possible. I really want you to know that you can do it at home when you have become skillful in this practice. This is my motivation to continue teaching. The only reason we aren't able to bring it into our lives is because we don't know enough yet or aren't practicing enough yet.

You may go on formal retreats to develop wholesome minds. But it is very important that you continue meditating outside of retreats because unwholesome minds arise in the absence of wholesome minds. Right now, as soon as yogis leave a retreat, they have no idea where all the wholesome minds have disappeared! It seems as if wholesome minds just arise on retreat, only to be replaced by unwholesome mind states as soon as a person returns home. You have to cultivate your own energy and your own wisdom. If you are suffering, you will need to sit down and work out what to do about it. If the parents always work things out for the child, the child will never learn for himself.

Finally, we all have to live, but we must ask ourselves: *Are we truly alive?* If we don't change and grow, it is akin to being dead. I encourage all of you to please continue practicing. I make an aspiration for all of you to practice at home and to enjoy the fruits of your practice.

When I know the mind is aware, there is a very strong feeling of goodness. I greatly wish for yogis to understand and appreciate fully the value of awareness + wisdom and their role in helping develop all of the wholesome qualities of the mind. This is the basic understanding that will carry the rest of the practice.

Mindfulness is a Lifestyle Change

When a retreat begins, defilements will negotiate with the yogi: "Okay, how long do you want to practice for? One month? Two months? Three months? All right. We'll leave you alone for that long. But when the retreat is over, then it's our turn again!" And it really is their turn again. Delusion loves hearing the line, "The retreat is over!" It is very common to think that *we've finished meditating*. When this happens, it is now time for defilements to come back out to play.

When I was younger, I went for long retreats of six to ten months at a time. My mind cleared up while I was in retreat but I stopped practicing back home and my mind went back to square one. My life did not change. I never listened to my teacher's advice to continue practicing at home and got into deep trouble! It was only when I was in the deepest trouble that I saw the need to work it out in daily life. I began to practice continuously at home and realized *the need to meditate all the time.*

When you return home, remember that you are there, at home. You should remain in the present moment there. The present moment is the

How can the Dhamma grow in us if we
are not always living the Dhamma?

only real thing. Stay where you are because the now is always now, there is no "after now." You're trying to have mindfulness in this mind and the only effort is to remember to be mindful in the present moment. Through everything in your life you are remembering *to* be mindful, remembering *how* to be mindful, and building and maintaining samādhi, or stability of the mind.

You use the information that you have, combined with intelligence, logic, and reasoning to figure out how to practice correctly. Next, you learn how to keep these already developed insights alive. Finally, you figure out how to develop even deeper levels of insight.

MEDITATING ALL THE TIME

We must be walking on the Noble Eightfold Path of sīla (moral conduct), samādhi (stability of mind), and paññā (wisdom). This particular aspect of meditation, where you need to be practicing it all the time for it to be alive and beneficial becomes apparent to someone who practices continuously. We really need to be a close friend of the Dhamma in order to grow in the Dhamma. It is when we are in such close communion with the Dhamma that we can grow in it. Otherwise, there is not much growth. How can the Dhamma grow in us if we are not always living the Dhamma?

The Buddha frequently reminded his followers to keep the Dhamma in mind. He didn't say *when* to have the Dhamma in mind, but just said to have the Dhamma in mind. Unless we are always meditating, delusion will step in and hold the door open for all the other defilements to move in.

People talk about how long they have been practicing meditation but they are only counting the length of time from their first retreat up to now. If they added up the hours that they were *actually* mindful, that would be a wholly different picture. The way we usually work is to put in a lot of effort over a small period of time in the hopes of getting some reward. That's greed at work!

Right effort is staying in it for the long haul. You need to become familiar with the work that you do, to always be in touch with it so that you become skillful at it. Right effort is not letting it slack off, not giving up, and never stopping. Keep going. That's real, right effort. Wisdom considers the long term. There's no hurry but we also do not rest. The more we understand the forces of nature and how they work, the more we begin to rely on the laws of nature to let things unfold in a steady way. It is also not for nothing that I'm using this word *nature* over and over. When something becomes your nature, *really* second nature, it means that the momentum of that nature is very strong in you. It has become your nature.

Momentum is important in every sphere of our lives and it is what makes things better and better. When there is momentum, it's not only easier to do what we have to do but also easier to grow our expertise and improve. If you were a high jumper, you would run to gain momentum so you can jump over the hurdle. Right now, you may run towards the hurdle, look up, realize how high it is, stop, turn, and walk back! You didn't have enough momentum to take the jump.

I would ask you to look at your mind right now. How often do defilements come in unnoticed? You've got to turn that whole paradigm upside down so that what is natural and unnoticed and always going on in your mind is *awareness*, *stability of mind*, and *wisdom*, just as the defilements are present right now. If you ask me about setting aside time for meditation, yes, we should do that. It is a time, whether we sit or use some other form, that we determine that we will have in mind to be mindful most continuously. When I was at home, I sat before I went to work in the morning and before I went to sleep at night. I also sat from time to time throughout the day in my shop or at the coffee shop. When there was a lull in my work or I had 5 or 10 minutes, I would be still and do meditation. All of these things gathered my mind.

We haven't reached the point where practicing continuously in daily life feels essential for us, so much so that we cannot live without it. If we felt that way about practice in our daily lives, we would maintain mindfulness so much more continuously. When we want to maintain the peace in our mind for longer and longer periods, we begin to realize that all these elements of knowing what we are aware of must become part of our practice and skill. Otherwise, we cannot maintain the peacefulness of the mind because we lose it when we lose awareness like a leaky faucet loses water. We leak peacefulness when we lose mindfulness while talking, walking or going about our daily business.

Let's use a business analogy to think about meditation. You secure some initial funding and you need to use your seed capital appropriately to start a business. So far, you have done retreats. Once the cash starts coming in, you learn to maintain that cash flow. In meditation, you now have to consider how to keep insights alive in your daily life. Do you know how to do that? To keep insights from fading, you have to allow these understandings to arise over and over in your mind. Continue practicing at home, as you would on a retreat. Once you can keep your insights alive and developing and keep your practice going, your business is now well established. You can grow it even more. You can dedicate yourself to expanding your business. If you do not, instead of being like entrepreneurs, you may be like day laborers who make just enough money to survive day-to-day.

Does all this discourage you or propel you to press forward and go the distance? Sometimes it is hard to tell yogis the truth because I worry that I might make it all sound too difficult! (*Laughs.*) But it's the truth. Can you imagine how much practice that is going to take? We want to turn the momentum of the current mind completely around so that it is going in the direction of wholesome momentum rather than unwholesome momentum. Now, when we look, it is natural for liking and disliking to arise. When we hear something, liking and disliking arises in the mind. That is natural for us now. Later, with more practice, it becomes natural for awareness + wisdom to be present when we look, hear, smell, touch, taste, or think. Then we can begin to trust that awareness + wisdom.

MAINTAINING A STABLE MIND

While I began practicing from a young age, I really started practicing at home in the midst of much suffering. I was in constant pain and sleep was my only rest. Every morning I woke up and the difficulty started again. I did not communicate much at the time. The only question I asked myself at that time was, "Why is the mind suffering?" This question really motivated me to keep watching the mind all the time. At first it was just suffering and I didn't know why. But slowly, from watching that

When you are aware of a peaceful mind,
it continues to be peaceful.

continuously, awareness and samādhi grew and the mind became more peaceful. There was less suffering.

When the mind began to have more peace then I made peace the main object for my awareness. Peacefulness became the anchor for my mind. Knowing the peaceful mind, I was also aware of everything else that was happening in the mind. I wasn't interested in whatever level of wisdom I had achieved; I understood that if I were mindful, there would be some relief. I knew that whenever I meditated, the depression was reduced a little. I understood that much.

I kept an eye on the peacefulness and on whether it was being maintained or disturbed with whatever contact there was with external or internal experiences. When you are aware of a peaceful mind, it continues to be peaceful. It becomes more and more peaceful. When you aren't aware of the peaceful mind then the mind starts breaking down into chaos.

How long can you maintain stability of mind in daily life?

The Buddha said that when there are leaves covering the surface of a lake, you can't see your reflection. Also when the water is turbulent, you can't see your reflection. It is the same with the mind. Stability and wisdom cannot arise when the mind is covered with defilements.

We give wisdom more opportunities to arise when awareness and stability of mind are present for longer and longer periods. Once you recognize the agitated mind and continue to know that agitated mind, it starts to become peaceful and clear again. Not being aware of the agitation or confusion only leads it to spiral into more agitation or confusion. When you know the peaceful mind continuously and you know everything that's happening in the mind, you'll also immediately notice when a speck of defilement comes to disturb that peace. At this point, you can immediately recognize the thought that preceded that shift from a peaceful mind to an agitated mind.

Sometimes, even if you're not watching a lot of objects, you can know the main object, which is the state of your mind. When you know the state of your mind, you also know the feeling, body, and mind simultaneously so there is no need to go after many objects. Instead, just know the state of your mind—whether it is peaceful or agitated. Keep that as your anchor as you know everything else and as you go about your business.

Yogis want to improve the quality of the mind but if you haven't seen the mind, the mind cannot change! In daily life, you may put in a lot of effort into your work with little energy left for awareness and awareness needs some energy as well. If you are not skillful at using just enough energy for awareness, you'll use too much energy and won't have enough to do normal work. Learn to use just enough energy, and then practice continuously. You will become skillful if you do this every day.

BECOMING ENERGIZED

It's very important to know the meditating mind that is at work because it allows us to see cause and effect and also helps us to continue doing the work. It strengthens and energizes the mind. Even when we observe that awareness is present, we must also be clear about the object it is knowing. Both must be clear in order to have a complete picture of the workings of awareness in the present moment and thus for wisdom to arise.

HOW DO WE MAKE INROADS?

For most of us, awareness + wisdom are not ready and on standby so defilements are allowed to arise over and over. It's a vicious cycle: we can't get peace; then we can't make inroads into the practice; so we can't get peace. Even if we forget about wisdom for a while, we are not even able to really continuously maintain just awareness and stability of mind in our lives.

Most of us become skillful at mindfulness of body and feelings but we don't become skillful with mindfulness of the mind. Particularly on shorter retreats, we do not become skillful in the third and fourth foundations of mindfulness—mindfulness of the mind and the dhammas. Short retreats give us time to calm our minds a bit and we go through the first and second foundations but we don't really get established in the third or the fourth. Then when we go home and stop practicing, and we have to start all over again when we return for another retreat.

When we are learning to be skillful at something, like putting in golf for instance, we putt again and again and assess whether the energy we have used is sufficient. We then adjust our game and try again. We need to bring that same approach to our meditation. Instead of a forced focus, it is a light attention and full interest in the process. People who cook will know what I mean. How will an extra onion change the taste of this dish? How would it taste if we were to cook the onion a bit longer? How would the taste change if we added soy sauce instead of salt? When we do everything else in our lives, we know how to use our intelligence to figure out how to do something best. Why don't we do this with meditation? Why do we just blindly follow instructions without getting personally invested and involved? If we get an instruction to focus, we may just start doing it without considering whether it is helpful. We need to assess for ourselves: Is this working? What is the effect? How is it? I want you to open the door to possibilities through your own understanding.

When I first began practicing, my teacher would ask me questions and leave them unanswered. I wanted to know the answers so I would go and observe in my meditation with his questions in mind. As a result, I learned. At first, it was just greed in wanting to know, and that didn't work! I then learned what did not work and what worked, and slowly found my way. I was fortunate in starting young and having a very good teacher in Sayadawgyi.

Skill and understanding of how to do right practice is very important. When we become skillful at observing **all** six of the sense doors and really have a handle on it, that's when we find ourselves confident about practicing at home in our lives. We don't know what circumstances are going to come up and we can't predict what people or situations are going to hit us.

I would liken mindfulness to a mother tending to a baby. Having children is a huge enterprise, as all mothers will know. I once observed a mother caring for her two-year-old and saw just how skillful she was with the toddler as he sat on her lap. She held a conversation with four

Whether it's action, speech or mind, there's some kind of idea behind these actions.

other people while feeding the child. As the toddler moved in her lap, she adjusted along with him, and every now and then gave him some food, and if he didn't like what she gave him, she would put the piece down and give him a different piece and later on pick up the original piece again to give the child. Sometimes she would eat it herself, always going with the flow, not making judgments of the child. Meditation is like this. We may find it difficult in the beginning to mind what we are doing and be mindful as well but it's all practice and habits.

INQUIRY AS A PART OF PRACTICE

If thoughts are too subtle, and you don't catch the thoughts, then the causes will not show themselves. So there can be *awareness* and *stability of mind*, but *wisdom* is missing from the picture. There needs to be a little bit of inquiry. First, we are mindful of what is happening as we move around in daily life. Then, later on, we'll begin to notice why our limbs are moving like that. There's a reason behind it. Whether it's action, speech or mind, there's some kind of idea behind these actions. There is no speech or action without some idea fueling it.

Why are you wearing the shirt you are wearing right now? Why did you place your keys, for example, over here, instead of in the corner somewhere? There are ideas in the mind. Notice what is happening. If you are at the point where you can be aware of the mind, begin to pay attention to how it is feeling or what it is thinking. You will then begin to see causes. The mind is knowing, aware and feeling. Pay attention to the mind that wants to do things or that wants something to happen.

These mental intentions are present everywhere in the body. What intentions are you aware of while you are walking? What are you aware of when you are sitting? What are you aware of when you are working? Do you notice the wanting to move? What do you want to move? Every movement involves mental intentions. If you're moving both arms, there are intentions involved in both of them. You can see these things if you're watching the mind. What are you aware of while you're reading this? If you only watch the body, you will not see a complete picture. When you begin to see a more comprehensive picture of how the mind and body are operating, then you will also come to see causes and effects and it becomes very interesting.

Defilements can still enter any time if there is awareness and stability of mind but no wisdom. So, even with the first two present, a little wrong turn in attitude can let in defilements! Fear can arise in just one thought. When you see one complete process, it will also be very clear that there's no need to go around in circles. The mind understands that because of this thought, this effect of fear happens. A yogi who pays attention to the way these causes and effects work will come to *own* this knowledge of cause and effect.

When I was trying to understand the emotion of anger, I asked myself whether I was happy or at peace when there was anger. *Why was there anger? What was I angry with?* When the mind is angry at something, there is some sort of underlying idea in there. The mind is holding onto a certain belief and getting angry over it. As soon as I saw this happening in the mind, the anger just slid away.

Sometimes people don't even have an idea of what they're angry about. So many things have accumulated over time that it's hard to pull apart the strands. It's all jumbled up. I sometimes ask people why they're unhappy and they don't even know.

You have to watch every time anger arises. This anger wasn't here a moment ago. Look at this feeling very closely. It has something to do with the conditions surrounding your experience at this moment because the mind has certain presumptions about these conditions. Is it a person? Is it something in the environment? Is it you?

For example, people feel that they shouldn't get angry when they're on retreat. Anger arises anyway. Now they're angry that there's anger! This is possible! Yogis then get frustrated. Sometimes the mind may be in a habit of getting angry at something specific so when this object appears, anger will arise. If you're able to understand this as a natural phenomenon, then the anger will go down in intensity immediately. How is that? It's because there is now Right Understanding.

You want to watch and learn what and why something is happening. You want to know why anger is present. Why does this feeling arise? Maybe you are dissatisfied. Why are you dissatisfied? You want certain things to happen. Let's say you don't get what you want or what you want to happen does not happen. You want something. Can you just watch this anger? It's impossible. The anger is going to keep on going. Why? Because there's some cause that you have not addressed yet. If you want to know the intensity of the anger, you can look to the *intensity of the wanting*. They are related.

When you have some preconceived notions about something and things don't turn out the way you wanted them to, anger will arise. Or you may feel justified in being angry over something. You may be relating an event back to a friend and you might say, "You know I really ought to be angry about so and so..." What does this mean? It's just the mind preparing itself to let this defilement loose. But it's never good to let anger loose.

GETTING IN THE RING

Now is the time for you to get into the boxing ring. I am the coach but all I can do is yell from the sidelines. For beginners, I'll shout strategies when you look to me for support. Amateurs will often look to the coach for further instructions while the old hands don't need to; they can think for themselves and deliver the punch. As a coach, I can yell what I want but you, as the yogi and boxer can only use the strategies you are familiar with. You are the boxer in the ring and you are facing the real deal.

When I practiced at home, I would talk with my teacher once every week or so. If you are practicing at home and do not have anyone to ask, ask yourself the question then set it aside. Later, consider what I've said and what the Buddha taught. What have you tried before? What has worked? Should you try one way or another way? Even those who do not meditate will sit down and really think through a life problem if it matters enough to them. The thinking we are referring to with meditation is not just random, abstract thinking but right thinking and use of wisdom.

My teacher never told me not to think. He didn't exactly encourage me to think either, but he did ask me questions that required me to be aware and to reflect on how I was practicing. I eventually discovered

When the practice becomes nature, it also becomes *your nature* to *understand dhamma nature.*

the answers and realized that one finds answers by being aware and by questioning. When you begin with the *why*, you are already bringing out your internal curiosity and intelligence. You'll have many questions initially in the learning phase, but you won't have that many in the wisdom phase. At that time, the mind will be clearer and less cluttered. The student is inside you. The teacher is also inside you.

"IF YOU LOOK AFTER THE DHAMMA, THE DHAMMA WILL LOOK AFTER YOU"

This work is possible. You need to be patient and work through it for a few years continuously and patiently. You need to taste the full flavors of Dhamma: of knowing, of awareness, and of understanding. You all have to cultivate your own energy and your own wisdom. When you have tasted enough Dhamma, it will lead you along. When I practiced like that, I finally understood the meaning of *if you look after the Dhamma, the Dhamma will look after you.* Or if you take care of the Dhamma, the Dhamma will take care of you. When you really practice long term, the practice just becomes nature. When the practice becomes nature, it also becomes *your nature* to *understand dhamma nature.*

Sometimes meditators are under the impression that they must practice in a specific way to get certain results. That's not the case. The process itself is a learning process. You are learning how meditation operates.

Take a Closer Look

My teacher constantly reminded me that all the problems in the world originate from the trio of lobha, dosa, and moha. Keep an eye on them. Watching and keeping these unwholesome qualities at bay will allow the wholesome qualities to arise automatically.

THE SPECTRUM OF WANTING

When there are lots of pleasant physical sensations, we may become greedy for more. Watch this greed while continuing to keep an eye on awareness as much as possible. When the wanting is very subtle and not detectable, you are at least still able to recognize the presence of awareness. With an awareness of awareness, it is harder for the mind to get lost in the pleasant sensations. Additionally, having to work at being continuously aware makes it harder for greed to wallow in the feeling.

Is a physical sensation of hunger in the stomach and wanting to eat the same thing? Without mindfulness, it becomes hard to disentangle these two and it seems like the same thing. As you practice more, you will begin to recognize the differences between a bodily function like the stomach growling and the desire to eat. When you are eating something, do you notice the difference between the taste of the hot-and-sour soup and the feeling that it is something pleasant? Hunger happens in the body or materiality whereas that desire to eat happens in the mind. That pleasant feeling is called vedanā.

Lobha entwines itself around an object. Will it wrap itself around an object and then let it go or will it entwine itself around an object and think, "*I can't let it go, I need it near me, I want it **all** the time*"? How strong is this lobha for this object? Let's say we see a flower growing on a roadside and some people may note that *it's a lovely flower* and keep walking while others may look at the flower and think that they want to keep it for themselves and pluck it. Some attachments are like post-it notes while others are more like superglue!

Let's deconstruct attachment down to its nature. You may be attracted to a particular person and you think you like the person as a whole. What exactly is it that you like about this person? Do you like their eyes or hair? Do you like the way they behave or the way they smile? Are you attracted to a mental quality? Do you have some idea about this person? Are they kind? Do they evoke a certain feeling that you do not get elsewhere? What particular characteristic is the mind wrapping itself around? Delusion can be so strong that we are initially attracted to a particular characteristic but as we are trapped and move towards the object, we come to believe we like the whole thing. Delusion spreads the view that *this whole thing is fantastic!* Only one or two characteristics reel us in and then delusion ensnares us whole. Check what catches your own mind and notice the experiences you are trying to recreate or re-experience through this particular product, person or experience.

THE WISH FOR EVERYTHING TO BE OKAY

Everyone has a lot of craving, but there is one very strong, but elusive craving. It is the desire for everything in life to be okay. This desire for everything to be okay is very strong and powerful, but we are not aware of it because it hits us at the subconscious level. We grow up thinking that everything must work out the way we want it to and become upset when something tiny goes wrong. The mind immediately becomes frustrated at the slightest hiccup. For example, if we want 10 things and we get all of them, the mind calms down without a problem. If we can't get one or two out of ten, the mind becomes agitated. If we can't get half, the mind goes into depression. If we can't get *any*, the mind may go crazy.

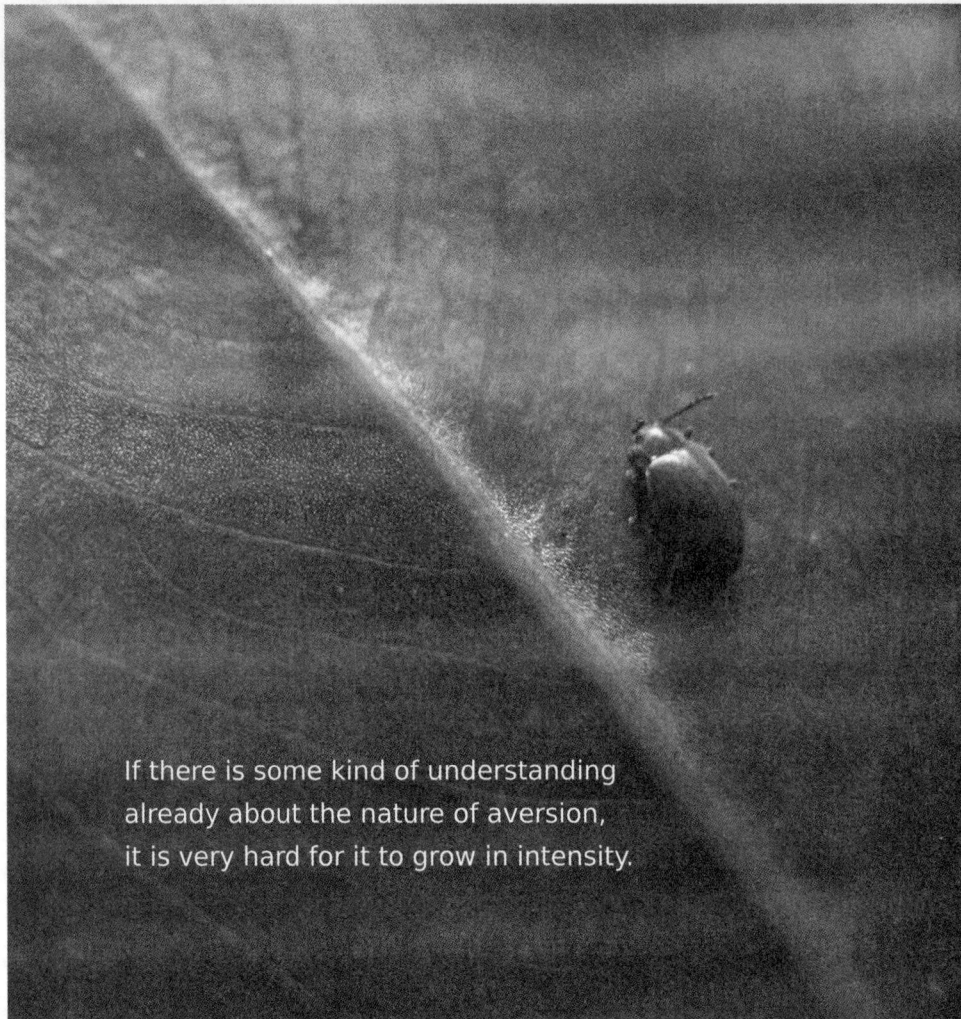

If there is some kind of understanding
already about the nature of aversion,
it is very hard for it to grow in intensity.

Don't expect that everything should be okay. The future is open and there is a 50% chance that the things that we do not want can happen to us. We need to be prepared for this eventuality. What is obvious is that we will age, become sick, be separated from our loved ones and die. Dukkha is certain.

WHY IS THERE AVERSION?

Let's talk about aversion and the gamut of emotions ranging from sadness, sorrow, and fear, to hatred, anger, ill will, and other forms of aversion. Why is there aversion? Why is it happening? Whose aversion is it? Study this emotion as it arises and as it is happening in order to understand its nature. If there is some kind of understanding already about the nature of aversion, it is very hard for it to grow in intensity.

When you are feeling angry about something, study all aspects of this anger each and every time it arises. Observe the feelings, thoughts, and anything else surrounding this anger. Observe the way the mind was thinking before this anger came up. If you become aware only when anger is already underway, or when it has passed, then you might not notice its causes. You need to see the train of thought that came before this emotion. By this we are not talking about conceptual ideas (i.e. "so and so is making me mad"). If you are aware of the mind directly while it is angry, you can see its causes. Pay attention to the thinking. What is it thinking? How does it think when there is anger? How does the mind think in the absence of anger? With such awareness, you will begin to see causes and effects.

So you see, it's not enough to just to *know* whenever something arises. You have to reach the point where you recognize cause and effect at work as well. Without catching the causes, the effects will continue to grow unhindered and anger will grow and grow.

Investigate these things and study the mind's phenomena at work. Recognize the internal chatter every time there is thinking. What kinds of thoughts are there when you are alone? What kinds of thoughts are there when you are with others? How does the mind think in these circumstances? *You need to see all of these things.*

ZERO TO ONE MILLION

There was a time in my lay life when I had been practicing continuously for a year or so and I hadn't had a major bout of anger for quite some time. I woke up sick one day and I went to work anyway and managed the family business alone. Little dissatisfactions accumulated throughout the day but I didn't take the time to work through them or clear them out.

Later that night, I asked one of my younger brothers (a doctor) for some medicine and he responded dismissively. That was the final straw. I just exploded, thinking, "How dare he talk to me like this?" I kicked a chair across the room as I was used to doing in my younger days. My family was all sitting around the room at that time and everyone looked stunned.

Awareness only kicked back in when my older sister asked, "What's happening to you with so much meditation?" I then saw the whole process internally and externally. I saw the frightened faces around me and realized how I had disrupted my surroundings. I also saw the whole mental process from a very tiny grain to this explosion. It became very obvious how negative this anger was. There was not one bit of wholesomeness anywhere.

Seeing all of this in one big picture, I made a vow that I wouldn't let something like this happen again. I learned not to continue along a line of thinking when I saw dissatisfaction arising in the mind. Instead I would switch to watching the feeling associated with that thinking. From then on, I would clear the anger out even when I noticed a little bit of anger. Nothing else mattered except to pay attention to even the smallest hints of anger and I would work with samatha (tranquility meditation) and / or vipassanā depending on the situation. Anger could go from a scale of zero to one and back to zero. I worked with zeros and ones, never letting it accumulate further.

Ask yourself *why* when you find yourself getting angry at something. Question why you continue to be angry and why you are getting even angrier. There's fuel somewhere. With many people, anger would go straight from zero to one to one million! Instead of cooling it with water, we're all dousing this anger with gasoline! So *whoosh, whoosh, whoosh*, of course it would grow!

DELUSION

There are always subtle defilements underneath and delusion is always there. Delusion is there whenever wisdom is not there. It is only in those brief moments when wisdom is present that delusion is not present. How many times does the idea of "I" not happen? You may notice it for a brief moment then delusion comes in to cover the wisdom up immediately.

Moha is darkness and you have a thief's tiny flashlight. When you turn it on, it will light up a small area in front of you and you're probably satisfied with that. You may think, "Oh, I know a lot now." What about everything that you do not notice? It's vast and you only know what you know, but you do not know what you do not know.

RESTLESSNESS

You don't need to try to restrict or rein in a restless mind. Just recognize that if the mind is scattered, that it is scattered. The fact that you recognize it means that something is already at work. Just know gently without getting lost in the thinking. The mind is like a monkey, going from tree to tree. How easy is it to control a monkey? Not so easy! Trying to control restlessness requires more energy and concentration, and will fuel even more restlessness. Remember that this thinking has nothing to do with *you*. You just want to know every time the mind thinks and be happy that there is awareness of this mental state. When the right attitude comes in and you acknowledge that a scattered, restless mind is not a problem, then the mind will become more stable.

If you know every time there is thinking, you (the meditating mind) don't get drawn into the thinking, right? You will get caught up in the thinking when you *don't* realize what is happening. Instead of taking the storyline as your object, just know that the thinking mind has arisen. When one new thought has happened, you know. When another new thought has arisen, you know. Many, many new thoughts will arise. Then you begin to observe that *the mind that you thought was yours is not yours.* The mind is mind, not "mine" or "me."

The real benefit of the Dhamma is
in having looked at defilements and
having understood them, to approach
the same tasks with wisdom.

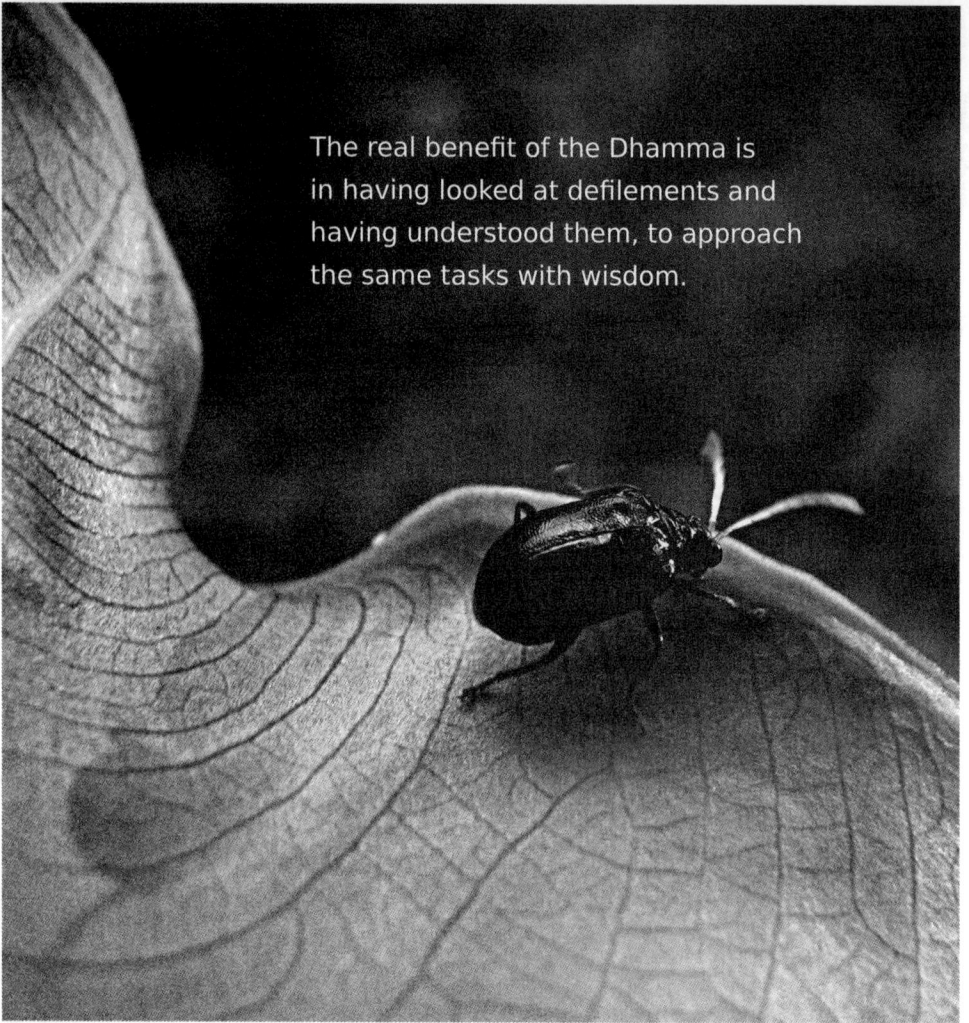

GOING THROUGH ROADBLOCKS

It's natural to have challenges arise in daily life and you may respond to these obstacles in different ways. You may solve the problem in the moment to make yourself feel better temporarily, but that brief relief won't uncover the Second Noble Truth or the cause of suffering. Remember that there is no flyover or underpass on the Noble Path; you have to go through town with whatever experience that arises. The lessons are all laid out for you, and you have to recognize it as a lesson, a chance to work with the obstacle and come to a realization that can free you. The real benefit of the Dhamma is in having looked at defilements and having understood them, to approach the same tasks with wisdom. We do not stop engaging with life issues. When the mind truly comes to understand something that is wrong as wrong, it will not repeat the same mistake again. Understanding will then mature and you can handle life issues wisely.

We want to realize that it is the mind and its machinations that make us unhappy. Some yogis tell me that they practice mettā to counteract judgments and comparisons but practicing this will not uproot the cause of suffering. Mettā is like a balm but does not take away the wound. It's more useful when you recognize how painful it is to judge. The purpose of living with awareness is to really know how things really are and to understand. Hopefully that understanding will free us from those defilements. So next time, do not use mettā as an antidote for that because then you won't see the truth of what is happening.

We should be interested in the relationships within us: the interplay of objects, the state of mind, wisdom, defilements, and awareness. These are the relationships that we want to take care of. People *out there* and what they are doing are concepts. Moreover, objects out there are not doing anything but minding their own business. But *this mind* is not minding its own business and getting into all sorts of trouble. This is the relationship we want to take care of and this is what the practice is all about.

Even if we were sitting somewhere and not speaking to or wanting to speak to anyone, we are still relating to our surroundings. Awareness should be observing this relationship. There is no need to fix the relationship that is already happening but we do want to be aware of what is happening. There is a temporary end to suffering and there is an ultimate end to suffering and we have to pay the price accordingly. Some things come easily and are cheaper. We will have to pay a higher price for something more valuable.

We should be interested
in the relationships within us:
the interplay of objects,
the state of mind,
wisdom,
defilements,
and awareness.

These are the relationships
that we want to
take care of.

Wisdom increases faith; anyone who understands the value of mindfulness and has benefitted from applying it in their lives sees their faith grow. The most important element of faith is faith in ourselves and in our ability to apply ourselves to the practice. Wholesome minds support each other just as unwholesome minds support each other. When there is more water, the fire goes out; when there is more fire, the burning continues.

Reflect. Learn. Keep Going.

Daily life will be full of ups and downs when greed, anger, delusion, and all their relatives come on strong. The wisdom you've got may not be sufficient enough to stop them. How do you approach such a situation? The first step is to accept whatever is happening in the mind *as it is.* Accept that this is just the nature of the mind. Unless you accept, you will be fighting defilements with defilements. I draw the analogy of try to accelerate a car with one foot on the brakes! The car won't move.

So, when you begin, the mind may not necessarily completely be open to this process. That's fine. This is how you start when you're developing your meditation skills. Learn from these different situations. Later on, you'll begin to notice causes and effects. Understanding the causes that lead to greater momentum in the practice will allow your meditation to improve naturally.

While something is happening, awareness will continue to collect data little by little in the background and wisdom will step in when there is enough data. When wisdom steps in, you will no longer continue with the unskillful action. Acknowledge and work through these challenging situations instead of avoiding them. When the mind comes understand that something that is wrong is wrong, it will not repeat an action again. The lessons are all there for you to work through.

What kind of understanding can you glean from what is happening? You can start by being interested. Then investigate. You will become aware of many different things but be mindful that these are just objects or experiences. Begin to ask more questions: What is a concept? What is reality? Continue to watch and learn.

Cultivate curiosity and interest—they are important ingredients. Don't be afraid of making mistakes, and never feel bad about having made a mistake. These false steps are the stepping-stones on our path and a part of our progress. We cannot avoid making them. Becoming aware of, carefully looking at, and learning from mistakes is wisdom at work! As we learn from our mistakes, wisdom will start coming in more naturally, more automatically. Over the years, as our practice progresses, as we become more and more mindful, the knowledge and understanding we have accumulated will naturally come in more quickly. Wisdom and mindfulness will start working as a team.

PAY ATTENTION TO SKILL AND RIGHT EFFORT

The dhamma encompasses everything. All the good and all the bad are all nature. You may only want the good and not the bad but that's impossible to have. You *will* have negative reactions. When there is insufficient understanding into phenomena or the wrong attitude towards an experience, you will have a negative reaction and you can't stop that. Just know that a reaction is happening. Know it and understand it, but don't try and stop it. Everything will fall into place once there is understanding. Wisdom will know how to balance, do what needs to be done and drop the unnecessary bits. Don't force something to happen. This goes against nature. While you can't get something just because you want it or you work for it, there are two things that will move us forward: *how much you do* and *how skillful you are.* Pay attention to applying skill and right effort— these pieces deserve your attention. Meditation is not like the lottery; you don't pay a little and win a huge windfall.

Reducing defilements is a learning process, and you will find that your understanding slowly emerges and moves toward the middle path as you recognize the extremes. Suppressing and expressing are the two different extremes, but you will experience them. Watch what the mind does in those moments, learn what is beneficial and adjust accordingly. If you

The defilement will
express the amount of
power it has and you
can't prevent that.

think something is good, you're at one extreme, if you think something is bad you're at the other extreme. You have to see things as they are and where they lie. Therein lies the Middle Way. For example, when a defilement arises in the mind, you neither try to stop nor encourage the defilement. Exercise right view in remembering that this defilement is not *you*. The defilement will express the amount of power it has and you can't prevent that. Just step back and keep an eye on the defilement, consistently and patiently, learning and figuring out how it functions and its job description. This is a learning process.

HOW TO WORK WITH DIFFICULTIES

How can we view the world through the lens of Dhamma? When we are thinking about the world, we are already thinking about concepts; we are thinking about people, places, and situations. When the mind pays attention to concepts, either wholesome or unwholesome states of minds will come up depending on how much wisdom we have.

I've noticed that when yogis observe defilements, it is often from a point of view that they are enemies to be fought. That is already a battle lost. Defilements like it when you fight because fighting in itself is a defilement and they like that they have a spy in your camp. Fighting anger with anger gets you more anger, or "anger-squared." Defilements cannot stand it when you watch them calmly. When you accept a defilement's presence, take interest in it, and try to understand it. That's when the defilement becomes really uncomfortable.

For me, I understood that difficulties would decrease if I practiced mindfulness. I noticed that the intensity of suffering and problems would decrease when I practiced. Truly understanding this motivated me to continue. When real understanding is present and strong, the mind changes for the better. If wisdom isn't strong enough, the mind can't change because defilements still arise. There are people who know about meditation but they don't practice; for these people, their minds do not really change.

Depression drove me to practice wholeheartedly at home. I remember first trying many different ways to alleviate these feelings. I went everywhere that I had ever been and explored new places seeking happiness but the depression followed me everywhere. I couldn't find happiness when I went out with my friends, whether I went to the beach or to the mountains or when I went thrill-seeking somewhere. Nothing made me happy. Even drugs couldn't do the job. It finally occurred to me one day that even if I were to go to the moon, the depression would also follow me there.

During this period in my life, my suffering became a very obvious object of meditation. I watched until it became unbearable and then I changed the object to something neutral to continue being aware. In Myanmar, ānāpānasati (awareness of the breath) was used as a common, neutral object but it was too subtle for me at the time because the suffering was so strong. I needed something stronger to make my breath obvious. I found the answer in a Vicks nasal inhaler because I found that when I used the inhaler my attention would be at my nostrils.

When it comes to using wisdom, I'm not asking you to think of a solution or to resolve the situation by thinking. That's not what I'm saying. Thinking a little allows us to practice effectively. I see it as a considered practice where you are aware and you reflect a little bit on what you're doing, how you're doing it, and what you're discovering: *a little bit*, not a lot. This is what we do when we are at work. When we do our work, we consider whatever work we have done before and how we accomplished this kind of work so we can figure out the best way to move forward. None of us do work without considering how to do it the best way possible. Even when we're trying to fix something we are not yet familiar with, we may tinker with it, take time to reflect, check what is happening, see whether it is working and then tinker a bit more. That is what I mean by using wisdom in using our own intelligence to find our way in our own practice.

If any of the Brahma Vihāras, or the "sublime states" of loving kindness, compassion, sympathetic joy, and equanimity arise, the mind will feel good and we will feel at peace and ease in understanding of the way things are. If there is compassion without wisdom, that compassion might actually be contaminated because it is mixed up with a non-acceptance of what actually is; a feeling of helplessness will be in there. If that happens, you will need to clear the mind first. Come back to observing the unwholesome mind state with right view. Do not try to force yourself to have equanimity. Work with the unwholesome states that arise until the mind comes to some balance. Then you will recognize whether it is any of the Brahma Vihāras arising in the mind.

DON'T LET GO OF MINDFULNESS

When I was deep in depression and I began to try practicing at home initially, I watched all my difficult emotions and it became a very strong motivation to keep awareness in order to get better. As soon as it got better I would lose the motivation to be as mindful. I would revert back to my old ways, talking and joking with neighbors and neighboring shops or customers. Then some trigger would hit me really hard, or hit a sore point that brought up all the old anxieties, fears, guilt or shame and I became overwhelmed again. Watching all the old fears and feelings would alleviate it a bit. But when it got better, I forgot again. It felt like people were coming by and slapping or hitting or punching me mentally. It was not intentional on their part; it was just that my mind was not strong enough to be resilient. Over many months, seeing the mind triggered daily and easily, I began to think about why I kept going back into this cycle. I suffered through this many, many times. I then realized that I was becoming too relaxed and not being mindful enough. When I began to feel better, I thought, "I can't stop being mindful." Even when I was feeling better and there was nothing to do, I would not waste my time talking needlessly, and I would always be mindful of something or another.

I became prepared when people came to talk to me. Other people can be full of defilements too and they come and unload their defilements on us. If we are not ready, we get affected and infected. Even with family members, I began to realize that I could not just relax. I could not drop mindfulness. My mindfulness got better and more continuous. This is how we learn from life—our failures and difficulties teach us.

Reviewing what goes on in the mind
is the work of wisdom.

REVIEWING WHAT HAS HAPPENED

My teacher would always ask how I was practicing and that is what I'm asking you now. *"What are you doing?"* or *"What is special or different today?"* were questions my teacher would ask me. Yogis who are practicing will know the answer while those who are not practicing will not know.

Reviewing what goes on in the mind is the work of wisdom. At first, when we watch anger, we are just watching. Reviewing what has happened sets a direction for the mind and creates a map of sorts for future awareness. You have a situation that you consider from different angles and decide to try meditating a certain way the next time. When the next time comes, you are more likely to remember to try it that different way. If you forget, set an intention to try again the next time. When you play a game with the same scenarios occurring again and again, you become an expert at knowing ahead of time what moves are beneficial and what are not at certain junctions.

If you want to improve, you first work continuously without a break. You also use the wisdom you've got, determining what is skillful and what is not skillful. You need to assess your practice for yourself. Like running a business, you've got to be savvy and learn from your practice.

Day-to-Day

When you are aware of what's happening in the mind, you begin to notice the undesirable parts and will want to change. This is a beginning. The lessons are all there for you to go through and learn. Later on, if you really come to understand that something that is wrong is wrong, you will not repeat it again.

> *Don't try to do anything,*
> *don't try to prevent anything,*
> *but don't forget what is happening.*

This is what my teacher, Shwe Oo Min Sayadaw would say as his instructions. In the first two lines, he is speaking to the experience of what is happening. Awareness can be at work, but you do not try to alter the experience. You let the process continue as it is without interfering. Let things unfold naturally. Your job is to watch, know, learn, and gain experience. As you watch an experience continuously, you'll begin to recognize patterns within it and later see the whole picture. The value of this meditation becomes more apparent with dedicated practice over long stretches of time. The more experienced you become, the deeper you will see. The dhamma is very subtle and you'll see this when you practice long term.

What is happening in the mind and what is happening in the body right now? How is one mind or mental state related to another mental state? You want to be interested in the nature of this mind and body. Hold concepts or story lines on the side for now. As wisdom gains traction and defilements eventually thin out, you'll see that there aren't that many *problems* per se. "Problems" arise when there is a lot of greed, aversion or delusion present. When we can't accept things as they are, we exhaust ourselves with desire for things that are not present or with desire to push away things that are already there.

The mind seeks variety, novelty and freshness and becomes lazy or bored when it's not satiated. If we think that a certain experience is lingering longer than we'd like, we're not observing properly. No two moments are the same. Every moment is fresh and every moment is changing. Even if an experience may seem neutral, we can still see subtle changes.

DOING WHAT SHOULD BE DONE

Yogis usually know about the Five Precepts and Eight Precepts so I do not need to tell them to you. If there is always mindfulness, you will automatically follow the Five Precepts. We must have some idea about what the Five Precepts entail in order to maintain them. It's important to have that kind of knowledge already, but I'm not the sort of person who wants to impose requirements on people. If you merely follow my instructions without conducting your own investigation, wisdom won't arise in you. You need to learn to the point where you personally understand why you need to act in certain ways.

There are two aspects of sīla or moral conduct: the doing of what should be done, and the not doing of what should not be done. If you know the Pātimokkha (the Buddhist monastic code), the Buddha says to *do good, avoid evil,* and *purify the mind.* The Buddha says to *do what should be done.* The Five and Eight Precepts that we always talk about is abstaining from that which should not be done. Remember that there is also the other side: *do as much as possible of what should be done.*

If we are being mindful all the time and wisdom is growing, we begin to understand what should and shouldn't be done, because we will observe the effects of our actions and learn from that. In my experience,

'Non-self' is just that principle of cause and effect.

my behavior changed through continuous practice. I became very calm and spoke very little or not at all if it was not important. I was serious when I did talk. Being very careful in speech became important in my practice. I practiced refraining from lying, slander, gossip, talking nonsense, speaking harshly, and idle chatter. And as a result, my meditation deepened.

CAUSES AND CONDITIONS

Every person acts largely out of their own past causes and conditions. People brought up in Asia have a certain cultural conditioning and people brought up in the Americas or Europe have their own kind of conditioning. Then there's individual conditioning, parental influences, and each person's experiences throughout life; there are so many combinations and permutations that everybody has a unique footprint.

'Non-self' is just that principle of cause and effect. For example, somebody may have a very hot temper, and that person's conditioning includes certain triggers that sets off their temper. If you understand that a person's past conditioning is what is causing them to lose their temper as opposed to believing that they personally have negative intentions towards you, then it becomes easier to see the process and forgive that person. You recognize that because of conditions, the results arise, and it's not the person who's angry, but a set of conditions that has brought about this effect.

If you stay in the present moment, moment to moment to moment, you see the principles unfold. If you are angry and you watch that anger many times, you will begin to notice how the anger cannot run away with you as long as you are aware. You begin to see how, with awareness + wisdom, the unwholesome mental states cannot take over the mind.

Without awareness + wisdom, the unwholesome mental states can gain momentum unbeknownst to you. When there is knowing, you begin to notice how the habit of anger could arise in the absence of awareness or wisdom and how the process unfolds naturally. It's all about mental processes; it's never about the story or external things. When you understand the benefit of something, the harm of the opposite becomes obvious.

I say this a lot: when yogis successfully observe something unwholesome and it passes, and they are happy. But that's not the end. It is important to reflect at that point what would have happened if we had not been mindful. If we are just happy in la la land we don't get to learn what it is like to be unmindful.

I usually tell yogis to stay away from the storyline, but it can help to see the idea that the story carries. The story might be, "Anne was making a noise and I felt really angry with her" while the idea behind that might be "people shouldn't make noise." This idea influences the mind. But when it is seen clearly for what it is, that this idea is not helpful, then it can be let go.

RELATING TO OTHERS WISELY

We get into a lot of trouble when there is attachment. When you or the other person is clinging to each other or to the relationship, *double trouble!* For example, thinking that *you will be okay only if your children are okay* implies that the mind is reliant on somebody else for its mood and that takes away the mind's freedom. This is a strong delusion. With attachment come anger, anxiety, fear, and doubt but if there's wisdom there can be loving-kindness, compassion, sympathetic joy, and equanimity. When the mind doesn't believe that its suffering comes from other people, situation or places, then it is free.

An old couple was once asked how their relationship had lasted 50 years. One of them replied that they made adjustments every time their communication broke down. It worked because that adjustment was not made with passion or defilement but with wisdom. We become strangers to each other in a family if we don't talk to each other for long periods of time. It takes a lot of wisdom to know whether and when to speak. Consideration of time, place, and other factors are all a part of that moment and situation before we can decide whether it is appropriate to say something. Sometimes it may be necessary to use humor to ease a situation; jokes and humor are very attractive to people.

So, love as much as you can but do not get attached. What emotions come up when you think about someone you love? If there is only love, there is only happiness. But love can get mixed up with a bit of attachment and that's followed by fear. Loss is a natural part of life so there will be loss eventually. We need to understand it instead of fearing it. Every day we are losing time, losing the object, losing awareness, in every moment.

SPEAKING MINDFULLY

We must be aware of ourselves every time we speak; come to know the many steps the mind goes through to speak. If yogis make a habit of knowing themselves, then awareness when speaking will naturally become part of that habit.

For some time I have had yogis not speak for two-thirds of a retreat and then, in the remaining one-third I explain how to be mindful while speaking and get the yogis to try mindful speech for a few days. Ideally yogis will have built up enough momentum and continue being mindful while speaking. But there is generally some inability or misunderstanding of how to remain aware when talking, and after a while I notice yogis speaking without being mindful and their momentum is gone. I now limit the practice to just one session to give just a taste of what it might be like to speak mindfully.

I did not invent this idea of cultivating awareness while talking. It is nothing extraordinary. The Satipaṭṭhāna Sutta prescribes, "When silent, be silent with awareness and wisdom, when speaking, speak with awareness and wisdom," but few people practice that. It's difficult to practice being mindful when speaking and seeing. The reasons are that we don't practice being mindful when speaking, seeing, and looking and we also don't have enough momentum in our awareness. The whole point of my retreats is that I'm teaching you a skill that you're supposed to bring into your life, and use in your life, so that mindfulness becomes a way of life. That's why I think it is useful to know and practice being mindful when you speak, especially when you are back home and at work.

The biggest trap when speaking
is the strong desire to speak,
wanting a lot to speak.

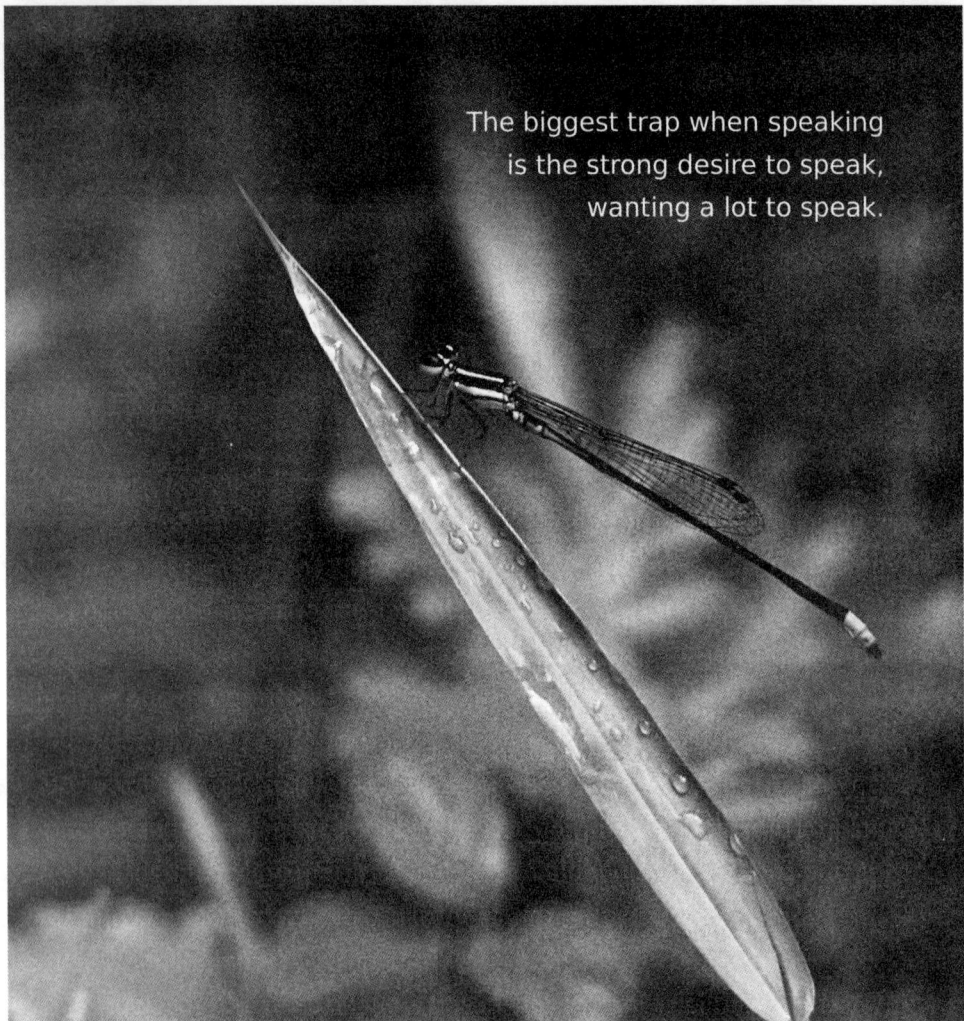

Awareness of speech is not a strange or wonderful thing but something very simple: be mindful when you speak. Some people ask, "What should I be aware of?" and I say, "Know that you are speaking, notice whatever part of the speaking experience is most obvious to you." On retreat we practice observing body sensations and feelings, and observing the mind. All these things are still present when we speak and we want to know which of these catches our attention as we speak. The biggest trap when speaking is the *strong desire* to speak, wanting *a lot* to speak. A strong desire to speak is *greed* and mindfulness then goes out the window.

We can't practice awareness of speech alone; we have to speak to *somebody*. We have to pay attention to an outside object, not just our own mind and body, so we lose mindfulness because our attention goes fully outside and then we are no longer attentive internally or to our speech. We start to think about the other person and look at the other person and then all our attention and our awareness goes outwards and our attention is no longer *also* directed toward ourselves. On the other hand, practicing talking meditation *too* formally and only in paying attention to one self will make the conversation stiff and unnatural.

A yogi said in a Finnish retreat that while the retreat is quite good for mindfulness, there's a lot of stuff happening and especially in speaking. When speaking with others, a yogi has to be responsive and quick and it feels like they're doing two jobs at once. Yes—it will be this way. It's all about skill, and skill is gained from continued practice. We will be slow in any subject when we are not skillful as yet. As we do it over and over again, we gain momentum and the process becomes easier. While there may be a lot of personal effort in the beginning, it eventually begins to roll on its own momentum, like riding a bike. I liken it to martial arts, where at first you are practicing some simple moves and after a while (you don't know when), you can just use them automatically. In this same way, the mind may now be a little slow and deliberate when it begins this practice, but as you keep doing it, you will find it slowly becoming automatic.

You could try practicing in *this* way: Know what you want to say. Think about what you want to say before you say it. When you acknowledge to yourself first, to what you feel and think before you speak, you are giving yourself time to know yourself before you speak. Try this over and over again. You can be aware of your experience as you are listening to the other person and recognize that you are listening. You are listening and knowing and are aware that you are listening and they are listening and then you are aware that the act of listening is happening, that speech is happening.

You might have to practice this quite actively; it *will be* difficult at first but only because you haven't had enough practice. Every new thing you learn is difficult when it is new because you don't have enough practice. When your overall mindfulness becomes more natural and continuous and has some momentum through practice and you know the mind and recognize it at work, it becomes easier to notice when you are talking. You will notice when the mind is thinking, when it is listening, when it is hearing, looking, and so on. You will need to accept that at first you *will* lose mindfulness quite a lot. Just don't give up.

Before I learned how to practice in social situations, I would spend as much time as I could by myself and did concentration practice. The mental stability was there but I couldn't find peace because I was resistant to social situations. I wasn't skillful but tried over and over again. As I learned to practice with people around, slowly over a long time, the mind's habit changed; my awareness increased and slowly became automatic. When I saw that my resistance was because of conditioning, I actively set out to practice in social situations to overcome the resistance.

At one point, I decided to practice right speech, meaning no lying, no harsh speech, no slander, and no idle talk. Taking on this task really helped me in talking meditation because I had to check if I was doing any of the four wrong speeches. It reduced the amount of talking tremendously and my practice just shot up because we speak so often and I had to be so mindful all the time.

I don't remember how long I practiced actively like this but after some time of practicing I could maintain my peacefulness while I was with others. After I was more settled, I actively increased the practice and sought out places that disturbed me because I knew that's where my weakness was. I would go to those places and keep trying there. Sometimes I would walk into a bar and meditate. I wanted to know how much this affected my mind and I became really interested. Everyone around me was drunk and talking loudly but I was very peaceful. This is how I developed confidence in my practice.

It's good to know, as information, that, *it is possible to be mindful when you speak.* Then you are willing to try and put this aspect of mindfulness practice into your daily life, to challenge yourself to use this as part of your practice.

It is very easy for defilements to come into our speech when we speak about ourselves, when the "I" becomes involved. At home we usually speak without mindfulness and it is this habit, rather than mindfulness, that tends to come in when we speak. When we are speaking, there are three things we can be mindful of: our mind, our speech and our body. If we know our mind then we should definitely be able to filter that into knowing our speech and our body as well.

SEEING IS DIFFERENT FROM LOOKING

You need to have your eyes open while meditating in daily life. I learned how to be aware with my eyes open because fellow shopkeepers used to tease me when I meditated at work with my eyes closed. They thought I was sleeping on the job! So I learned to pay attention to the internal landscape while keeping my eyes open. I eventually became more skillful at knowing the difference between seeing and looking, and the people I worked with didn't even know that I was meditating.

If you actively know that you are aware and you are tuned into this awareness, then it's hard to miss the seeing that's happening in this moment. One exercise you can do to help recognize this is to sit with your eyes open when you do sitting meditation. Be naturally attuned to your internal landscape without bringing your attention to your eyes. While this is happening, attention will naturally stray to the process of seeing and you will know that seeing is happening. It can be those moments

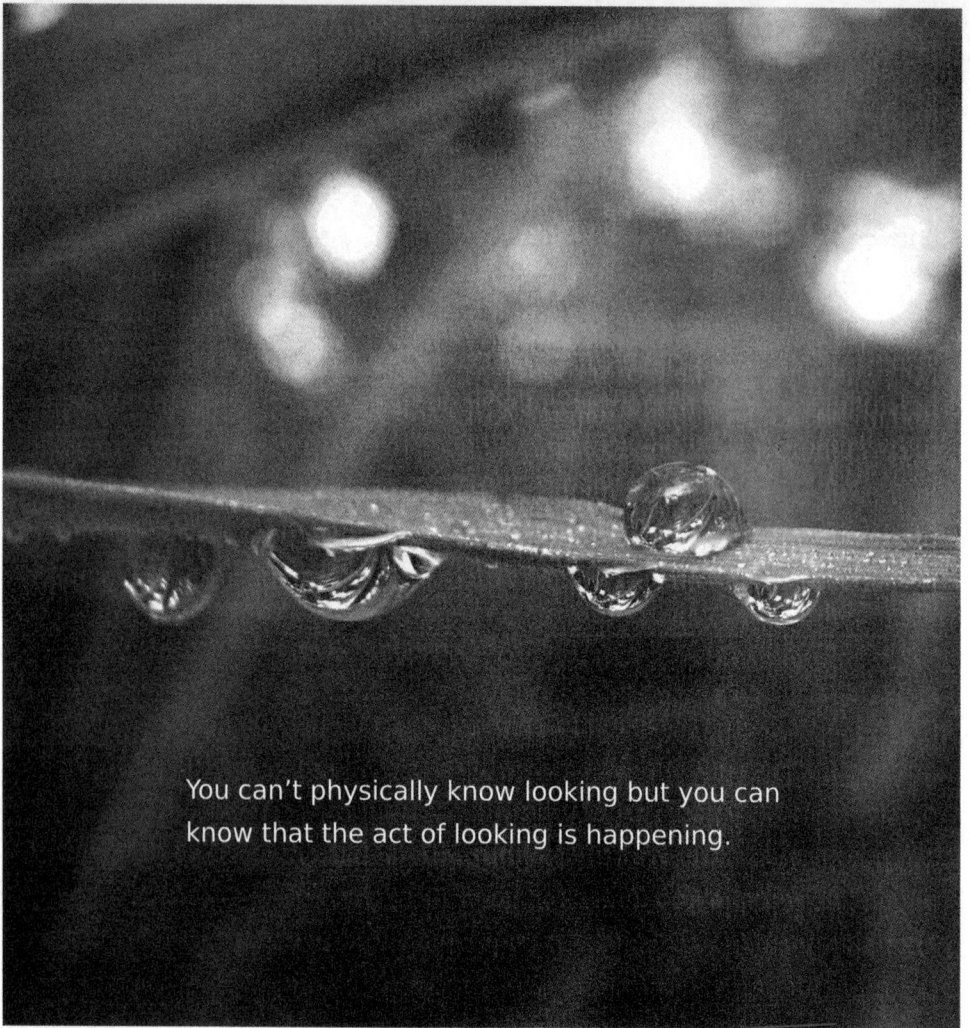

You can't physically know looking but you can
know that the act of looking is happening.

when the awareness naturally settles on seeing and it can hit us with clarity that seeing is happening right now and being known.

When we do not understand the reality of seeing, then sometimes putting attention on our eyes gets us lost in the *things* we see instead of recognizing that seeing is happening. Sight or seeing is such an obvious object that we do not recognize it as such, simply because we don't yet understand its mechanisms.

It's a similar story with the act of looking. We want to pay attention to the mind that is doing the work of focusing on seeing in order to pick up something visually or to use certain information in order to function. You can't physically know looking but you can know that the act of looking is happening. It's not something tangible but you can know that it is happening. This is because reality is not solid. We can understand reality or we can know reality but that's all we can do. If we are able to be aware of awareness, able to know the mind that is doing the work of being aware, then that awareness will pick up seeing or looking on its own. These little skills are necessary, particularly in daily life.

THE PROCESS OF EATING

All six sense doors are working while you're eating. Do you know everything that is happening? If you forget yourself while you are eating, there will be a lot of eagerness there. Eating often has a kind of excitement and eagerness that accompanies it. So before you start eating, check and see if there is eagerness. When this excitement calms down, awareness will become steadier.

Taste arises on the tongue. Where does the feeling that *this food is good* arise? In the mind! They're wholly separate. Of course when we speak, we say, "This tastes good." You'll have one and the same durian but some people will like it while others can't stand it. Durians have this one taste but the idea that this durian is either "heavenly" or "disgusting" happens in the mind. There was a Singaporean yogi who did not like durians and he watched the disliking mind. When the disliking passed away, he then tried the durian. Now he likes durians!

Taste has nothing to do with it. Some of you probably were turned off by the smell of durians from the very beginning. The first whiff made such a negative impression on the mind that it labeled everything about the durian as negative, beginning with that initial association with the sense of smell.

So, let's relate this to your daily life. When you are outside and you judge a certain kind of sound as distracting or bad, then perhaps you will go looking for a place where there are no sounds. Can you find any place without sound? You have to understand the nature of sound. You may consider a certain kind of sound *noisy*, *distracting*, or *bad.* You may then go in search of a place without sounds. But can you find any place that is completely silent?

THINKING PROCESSES

We need insight into the nature of the thinking mind because much of our suffering comes from thoughts. Have you ever thought, "What if this car gets into an accident?" How did that feel? There is fear when "I" is involved but the mind is free when it knows a thought as just a thought.

Thinking in the right way is part of the practice. Yogis are often afraid of thinking about meditation but in fact, to do any kind of work, we need to consider the situation, reflect, and think. We use wisdom to make fewer mistakes and we actively reflect on meditation work that's productive and useful. This helps us recognize what's helpful in our practice and strengthen that. What we are observing, experiencing and thinking about how to practice, it all comes together.

The thinking mind in itself is neither wholesome nor unwholesome. It is the *motivation* of defilement or wisdom *behind* the thinking mind that determines the quality of the thought. We are concerned with *this quality* of mind. Naturally arising thoughts are not a problem because they are just objects to be known. Of course, if there is a defilement, we ought to deal with it and not let it carry on unchecked. If, on the other hand, it is wholesome, we can encourage it.

It is best not to observe the thinking mind alone. Also watch the feelings that accompany this thinking so that you can know when it is becoming too much. You can also gently allow the overthinking to continue and learn from it. You will experience when it has become too much and having this experience will allow you to learn from overthinking.

When there are strong wholesome qualities in the mind, it is difficult for the mind to suddenly change and become unwholesome; when there is a strong unwholesome train of thought going on, it's difficult for it to suddenly switch and become wholesome. I experimented for myself when my mind was wholesome. I tried to intentionally think negative thoughts and realized that I could not.

Know that not all Dhamma-related thinking will necessarily be wholesome. Sometimes a self-righteousness or attachment will be fueling it. When Dhamma-related thinking has to do with your actual practice, it's probably helpful. It's helpful to think about the Dhamma and it's okay if you don't understand things straight away. The Buddha recommended this kind of consideration because you never know when the mind might be in the right state and suddenly understand! Take in enough information to help you understand whether this information is beneficial, suitable, too much, too little, or balanced.

If you can see the wanting to think, know that. Observe the intensity of the wanting. When, through skillful observation, the wanting diminishes, the thoughts will also diminish. If you can't see the intentions to think just switch back and forth between thoughts and body as objects.

LOST IN THOUGHT

Do you know that you are walking when you are walking around in daily life? You will often be lost in thought. If you realize that this is happening, just know, "The mind is thinking." What is important is what is happening in this moment. You can do what you need to do when you arrive at your destination; there's no need to think about it now. This way the mind will also think less about the future. You can expend a lot of mental energy speculating about the future without actually knowing what is going to happen. If you discover a very different outcome than what you had expected, you have spent a lot of energy on imagination!

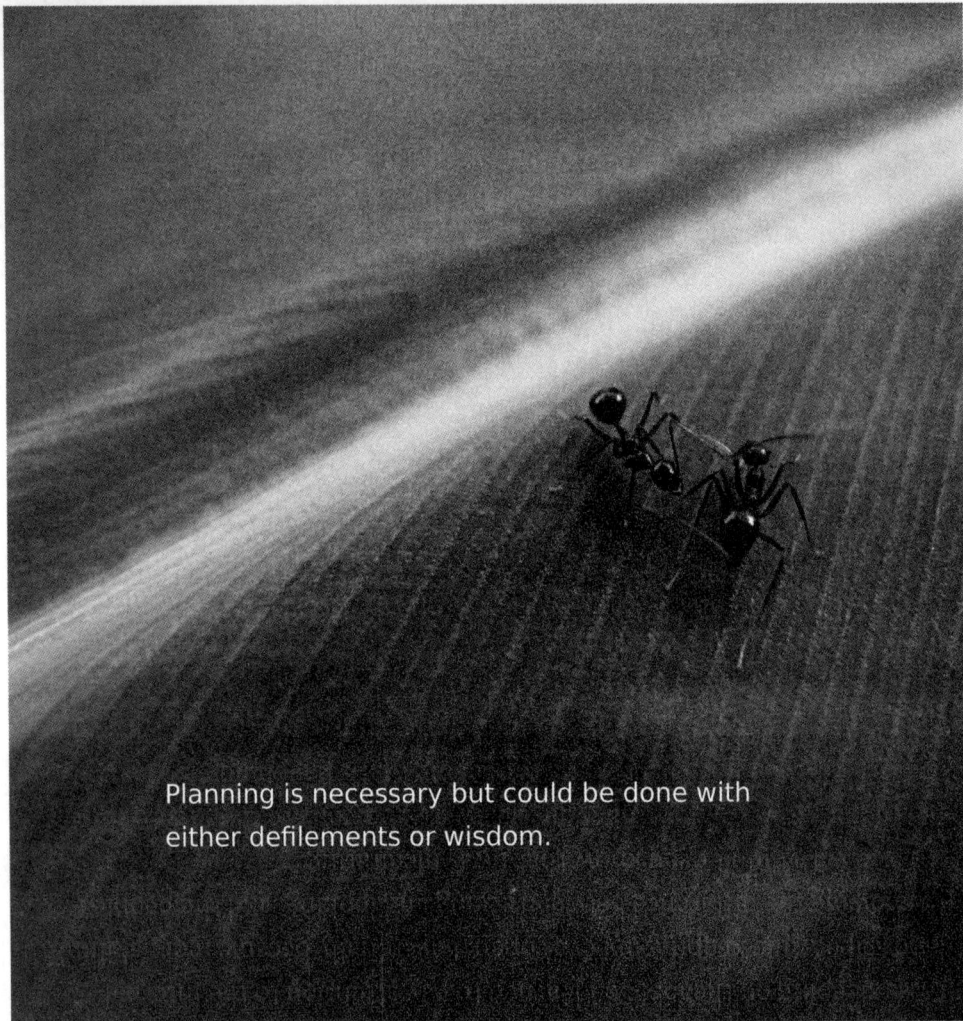

Planning is necessary but could be done with
either defilements or wisdom.

There was a businessman who went to the market to buy goods wholesale to resell later. His journey to the market was filled with thoughts of various prices, how he would try to get there before everybody to get the first pick of goods. When he arrived he found there was nothing there for him! This businessman was a yogi and so he was aware of what his mind was doing this whole time. He realized how much time he had wasted speculating and determined that on future market trips he would relax and make decisions when he arrived.

MEMORIES AND PLANNING

The concept or story is about the past or future but the knowing of that is in the present moment. You need to consider how you might respond to a certain situation so that you arrive prepared, but this is not the same as worrying about a situation. If you are planning and knowing with wisdom that this is happening, that's the present moment. Planning is necessary but could be done with either defilements or wisdom. Do you worry when you're planning? Some people plan with greed and others with anxiety but there is a way to plan and think in a relaxed way.

Thinking about past events will also happen naturally from time to time and there's nothing you can do about it. You can't go back and change the situation. You can only revisit the past in thought. However, you can learn a lesson and not repeat the same mistakes. One yogi realized that the idea of "one second" of time was a concept and the past dropped away for him with this understanding.

AWARENESS AT WORK

Meditating at work is a skill and by skill, I mean lots of practice! Initially, of course, when you pay attention to *outside* phenomena, you can't concentrate on phenomena *inside*; when you put your mind inside you can't really be aware of what is happening outside. Initially you might not be able to be aware of inside and outside when you are working but try to practice whenever you can to allow momentum to build. At some point awareness will kick in naturally while you're doing something you're really absorbed in. Getting to this level of awareness requires consistent practice.

When you need to be working, just do it fully. Sometimes you will have more time to devote to your practice and do it freely and you will know something like, "Oh the mind is thinking about this so it can do that." When you build the habit of noticing the mind at work then you will notice that awareness just starts popping up because it becomes a habit for the mind to recognize itself doing work. This will just come in naturally. Allow this to happen.

A yogi once asked a question about building up continuous practice, "How much should we do?" I said, "Do it 50-50." The yogi was a psychiatrist so he thought a moment about my suggestion and asked, "How do you measure?" (*Laughter.*) I considered it and realized that it wasn't as much about a division of *50-50* as much as allowing the mind to do its work naturally. If it is very practiced then the knowing happens naturally.

When you have a continuous practice that reminds and remembers and knows the mind at work, then it gets to the point where it becomes *effortless* because the mind becomes so familiar and so intimate with itself. It is always with itself and it likes being with itself. That's when it allows the mind to do anything because it doesn't mind; it's always with itself. The operative word is *continuously*. Although it is difficult in the beginning, any amount of effort you put in brings momentum and that in turn makes it more effortless and continuous in the future. That's why the Buddha said to practice continuously.

WHEN THE MIND SAYS, "IT'S NOT FAIR."

When something happens, the mind starts making judgments, sets up parameters, and develops ideas of what's appropriate and boundaries of "you" and "me." Once hooked on these ideas, the mind won't like it when one of these ideas is violated.

We encounter this all the time. In Western society, people wait in a queue or line because there is a belief that people should wait their turn for something. There is a dissonance when someone cuts that queue/line and thoughts that *they should be in* line start coming up. Or different thoughts of fairness might come up. There could be another kind of belief, "I wanted to get to my food and she has slowed that down by jumping the queue." The mind has convinced itself of all these strands of thought! At times like these, we should ask ourselves, "What internal belief is being thwarted here?" Right now, someone's actions are frustrating these beliefs and the mind justifies this anger against the other person!

STRINGING EACH OTHER ALONG

In daily life, we give each other compliments and thank each other for their compliments. We string each other along by reinforcing the need to look good and feel good. If instead we had said, "You look really terrible," the listener might get irritated because people want to feel good. We are often at the mercy of other people's words, compliments or insults and are generally automatically affected. When there is an understanding of how these thoughts work in the background, the wanting will disappear.

FEELING LIKE BEING TAKEN ADVANTAGE OF

It is very important that there is a right attitude when we are working in the world. Sometimes we may feel like we are being taken advantage of or being taken for granted. How different would it be if we thought these people were acting in a certain way because they didn't know any better? If someone were bullying you, it would be really tough to handle! You may get tense, agitated or angry with the bully. What if you thought that this person was only inadvertently doing these things because she didn't know better? How would you feel then? You can better understand and forgive.

SELF-JUDGMENTS

"Bad" is just a label. Don't label yourself that. When the mind is wholesome, the person is good and when the mind is unwholesome, the person is bad. It's only for that moment and that's always changing. Continue to practice and take your time; the fact that you are practicing shows that your mind wants to become better and that means that the mind *will* become better.

How do you experience silence?
How do you experience the stillness
of a garden or the woods?

When doubt is strong in the mind, do not pay attention to these thoughts. Once we give attention to these kinds of thoughts, they suck us in and grow. We can anchor ourselves to feelings instead and not give any power to the conceptual thinking. Follow the same principle for other strong, unwholesome states. When we look at the feeling and discontinue looking at the thoughts, it will help the mind calm down. Then we can look at these thoughts and feelings together when we feel we're ready.

Everyone has his or her own path and there's a natural course that needs to unfold for each person. You can watch what's happening in the mind and understand it, but you can't force it. You may learn a technique at a retreat, but it is when you go home that you can apply that technique all the time. That's when your life changes.

PRECONCEPTIONS

How do you experience silence? How do you experience the stillness of a garden or the woods? I've asked different people this question. Fear comes up for some people. Youngsters tell me that they get bored when there's nothing to occupy them. As you can see, *good* or *bad* depends on the person experiencing it, depending on their preconceived feelings of it.

There are tons of these accumulations that you have from childhood and you really want to see these ideas that have built up over the years. If these little preconceptions are seen properly, then the mind will no longer be disturbed by what is happening. If you continue to meditate regularly, there ought to be fewer and fewer attachments.

GIVING COMES IN DIFFERENT WAYS

The market where I had my shop was a very busy place. Lots of shops were lined up side by side with narrow alleys between them. Shopkeepers sent goods in and out with carriers who ran back and forth for the shopkeepers. People would run quite blindly, not caring who was in the way. I would get irritated whenever I had to get out of the way, which was quite often! I knew that people would run into me if I didn't move aside, but also became annoyed that I was the one who always had to be careful. This was a daily occurrence.

When I began to practice continuously, I became mindful of my irritation with this market situation. After being mindful of it regularly for a long time, I actually began to see it as a good practice to give space to these people to prevent accidents and I saw moving aside as a practice of generosity. As I practiced day after day and mindfulness arose, good actions also followed. The aversion that accompanied the critical mind decreased. With aversion gone, I began to feel mettā for these people.

DIFFERENT EXPERIENCES, DIFFERENT REACTIONS

When necessary, use every weapon you have in your arsenal.

There will always be some kind of contact at the six sense doors. Don't follow any such contact. Just know the state of mind and stay with the knowing, observing mind. How does the mind feel or react every time there is contact at the sense doors? Is there a resistance? You may not necessarily let go and accept the situation initially, but that's fine because you are using this experience as a tool to develop skill in meditation.

In daily life, where wisdom may be weak, you want initially to pay attention to awareness. The mind can recognize the situation happening while awareness naturally collects data in the background. As awareness picks up more data from the experience, and the picture becomes complete and wholesome minds grow stronger, you will eventually stop acting out of defilements.

Let's say you are in a social situation and you have accidentally said something harsh because there was too much momentum to speak. Let awareness continue to know in the background while you're talking to others. At some point of seeing this whole process, awareness will have enough of a picture that wisdom can arise and resolve the situation. It is inevitable to make some wrong turns in daily life but you have to learn how to profit from these experiences. Don't allow defilements to run freely or your situation will deteriorate.

Imagine the alternate result if only delusion were operating. Perhaps that situation would become exaggerated. We have to recognize things for what they are. If the mind has a bad habit, we have to recognize that. There is awareness so you're keenly aware of what goes through your mind. It takes time and everybody has different characteristics. We all have faults and we need to look at what is in our mind and know it until the mind realizes that it doesn't want to be that way anymore. That realization will help you learn how to let go.

We think that there are many people that we interact with in our daily lives. In fact, most of us will usually interact with a certain limited set of people over and over again. How do we work with this? How can we strategize so that we become skillful? So long as there is the intention to have the Dhamma in our lives, then it will become easier.

Having these experiences is very important and each experience gives you a life lesson. It's like playing videogames, which I like to talk about with children. You work at it and reach the first level. You graduate to higher and higher levels and eventually win the prize. You know how to do this because you've got that experience. You know how you can win this game at this level. Of course if you don't know how to learn from your experiences, you won't get anything no matter how many life lessons come your way!

We all have faults
and we need to look at what is in
our mind and know it
until the mind realizes that it
doesn't want to be that way
anymore.

That realization will help you
learn how to let go.

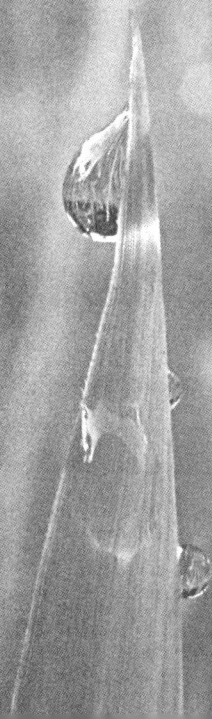

We are not patient with gentle awareness;
we do not believe it will work or trust that
it will grow into something.

A Lighter Approach

When I began to meditate in earnest at home, my awareness was inconsistent. I over-compensated for this spotty awareness by putting in a lot more personal effort. I wanted to be as mindful as possible but I was just too tired to do any more than that. Even then, there was only so much I could do. After some time, I began to notice a lighter, general, but discontinuous awareness that, done day after day, formed a pattern of long-term practice. The momentum that came out of general awareness created these dots that came together to form a tsunami of awareness that could be seen clearly.

We do not believe gentle awareness will work or trust that it will grow into something so we are not patient with gentle awareness. Personal effort uses *our own* effort while waiting patiently for momentum to grow uses a natural process, a natural law, and natural energy. Unfortunately, personal effort is short-lived and does not allow us to function in the day-to-day. We then begin to doubt our ability to live our lives with awareness.

The idea of figuratively *looking lightly out of the corner of your eye* describes a kind of awareness that watches the workings of the mind in its receiving state. The mind becomes aware of all the objects that match this mental frequency. Alternatively, when we turn and pay attention solely on the objects, and make too much effort to see these objects, it will feel like the objects have disappeared because the observer and observed are no longer at the same frequency. We can use an analogy with the optometrist here. When you go to the optometrist, they might have you try out different power lenses to determine what would work for you. When the power is right for you, then you see the letters clearly. When the optometrist tries out a power that is too low or high, the letters on the chart become blurry. It's the same deal with the mind that is at the right frequency with objects. While you may assume that putting in more personal effort will yield better results, you may still not be able to see clearly.

A light, general awareness allows us to continue functioning, to do the activities we need to do while a light recognition of what is happening works steadily in the background. This very gentle awareness, while not continuous in the beginning, will eventually gain momentum. When it becomes a natural, continuous awareness, it will really feel like you're aware and you'll feel like you're living this awareness in everything that you're doing. For me, it was at this point that I really understood the true nature of vipassanā meditation and began to believe that it is possible to become enlightened while living life.

USING WISDOM

Meditators often forget to use their natural wisdom when they meditate at home because they haven't practiced using it. Investigate and use your wisdom to check in on whether awareness is present and how much effort is being used instead of blindly putting in more effort. Here are some considerations: *Can you see your level of effort? Is there stability of mind? Do you know what that experience is like? Do you know your level of confidence or faith? Is wisdom at work?* Meditators can normally recognize when there is awareness. However, fewer meditators can recognize wisdom at work.

Wisdom is one word but it operates in so many ways.

Sometimes we miss the fact that wisdom is there and doing its work because we aren't familiar with the ways of wisdom. We are not close to wisdom like we are close with close friends. We're more familiar with effort. I see meditators trying hard to stay awake. When we are sleepy we should instead do a bit of investigation of this sleepiness. *Why is*

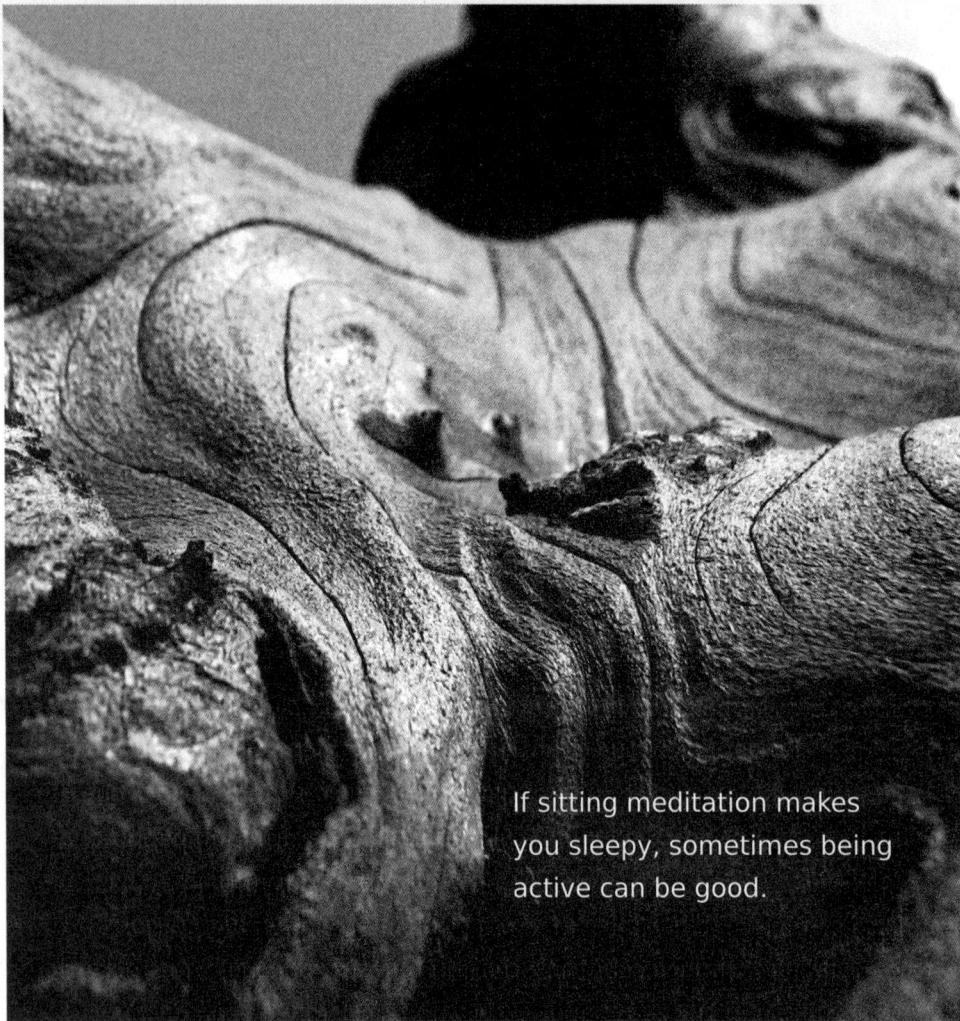

If sitting meditation makes you sleepy, sometimes being active can be good.

there sleepiness now? What has brought it on? What does it feel like? Instead meditators react negatively to sleepiness. They will try different tactics to fix the sleepiness instead of seeing it as it is and learning more about it. I see this playing out in the dhamma hall during sitting sessions. Some meditator starts falling asleep and the expression on his face shows that he is unhappy with himself as he picks himself up. Blindly continuing these actions could just form bad habits.

If sitting meditation makes you sleepy, sometimes being active can be good. If you give the mind work to do, if it is being actively aware, then it will be alert and awake because it is doing something. You can also try sitting with your eyes open.

We need to use wisdom the way we use our intelligence to solve problems, grow our businesses or think through what needs to be done at home and at work. In daily life, we figure out how to do things, consult with the right people and strategize to make a profit. We need to recognize the presence of wisdom and apply similar skills to meditation.

PROBLEM-SOLVING FOR YOURSELF

I often circulate around the Dhamma Hall of the Shwe Oo Min Meditation Center in the afternoons. There was a nun who sat right up front and I would see that her face would turn pink, over and over again. Later in the interview I asked her why she was blushing repeatedly while she sat. She said that it was because of her body's tendency to pass a lot of wind and she felt bad for the person sitting behind her, every time! So she went red in the face when her body did it again. I asked, "So what are you doing sitting in the front of the hall? If you are concerned and if this is what your body does, sit at the back of the hall! The door is wide open and you don't have to sit in front." This meditator felt that she should have been sitting up front because she was a nun. We cause ourselves trouble with our beliefs. Suppressing such bodily needs can be uncomfortable and eventually make us sick. Instead, we can find alternative solutions.

Set yourself free! Do what you need to do to meditate instead of holding certain ideas in your heads without considering an appropriate solution.

CREATING A DHAMMA COMMUNITY

Before I began meditating, I was the black sheep of the family. My words carried little to no weight because I was known to lie about things. But about three years into my practice, I spoke less and less, as I watched my speech very carefully. By then, everyone would listen whenever I spoke because what I said was something of value. They listened because they knew that what I said had a lot of thought behind it. Sometimes my family would be unnerved because they knew what I was saying to be the truth.

My family had regular Sunday social get-togethers where we would eat and then talk. The conversations usually revolved around the latest cars, movie stars, and such. I had been meditating for some time by then and found this to be a waste of time. I considered what could be done and slowly an idea formed in my mind. One day I suggested that we all meditate together. All of us had meditation experience because my father used to bring us all to the monastery. So they agreed to meditate. We all sat for 15 minutes initially and then we would eat.

After a while the idea crystallized, and we sat together in meditation every time we met. After eating or during the meal I then suggested a discussion and we would talk about life, whether we were happy or unhappy. I would ask them one by one, "How do you feel about your life? Do you feel satisfied with your life?" The party would turn serious; one brother replied that he was not satisfied with his life and another replied that it was *50:50*. Slowly my siblings began to share the details of their lives and feelings, and someone would cry after sharing and get some relief. It was not something they had considered. Everyone was just sort of going through life, time was passing by, and they'd never given any thought to how they were living their own lives.

From one week to the next, the questions would continue: If you're not happy with your life, how do you make yourself happy? How do you deal with it? We brought the Dhamma into the conversation and it turned into Dhamma discussions.

With wisdom, you will also know how to help others.

Everyone was just sort of

going through life,

time was passing by,

and they'd never given

any thought to how

they were living their own lives.

*I want yogis to know that mindfulness is a
lifetime commitment, not part-time work.
It is something that we really need to do all the time.*

*Only when we see the nature of the mind
will we understand the nature of dhamma.*

Continuing the Work

CAUSE AND EFFECT CHAIN

A yogi in one of my retreats had some questions surrounding free will. When we talk about the process of conditioning, remember there's a stream of minds in the conditioned process. The conditions in one mind bring the effect into the next mind and then, whatever the mind chooses to do in the next moment adds a little to that quality, or takes away from that quality. It then passes away and then this condition gives rise to the next mind and then it passes away and the effect is given to the next mind. Every mind begins with something, a condition, but that mind has a moment in the present to choose its contribution to the moment in terms of action or non-action, before that mind passes away. "Everything is conditioned" just means that there is a stream that's going on and the present moment has been conditioned by the past. At the same time, there is an element of choice in the present through wisdom because wisdom has free will. As a result, that wisdom has the ability to choose to take whatever action or non-action it would like. All things are conditioned but also you cannot imagine the vastness of kamma that you have accumulated that has the potential to flower in every moment.

If somebody has developed a lifetime habit of anger, the person will become angry with a little trigger. If the person has studied meditation, starts practicing and understands the benefits of meditation in the present moment, this person may gradually develop to the point where, with awareness + wisdom, the person may possibly be able to consciously decide what to do. This person could decide whether to continue to be angry, on the one hand, or try to be aware of the anger and grow in wisdom as a result, on the other. This choice constitutes free will.

If only delusion were present, then the conditioning is set and this person would act entirely according to that conditioning. When this kind of mind is not interested in wisdom, the mind is just a push-button system that is triggered by external forces. Conditioning will dictate all outcomes.

Awareness allows the mind to choose. You might hear someone talk about something or you might come across a book that opens up a bit of wisdom. You may borrow some wisdom from a book or person, consider it, and apply it to your life to bring about more wisdom. In this way, we can see how awareness + wisdom yields freedom of choice.

While I've said all this, I also don't advise yogis to reflect too much on these matters. It's easy to get lost in conceptualization and abstraction on these topics, and thus to drift far from the present moment. One of the conditions for wisdom to arise is to think deeply about the Dhamma, but it absolutely needs to be grounded in Right View and Right Thought.

BUILDING UP INSIGHTS

When we are experiencing an emotion, we can both be with the emotion and understand the nature of the mind that is feeling aversion or craving for this emotion. This is a more powerful realization than just being relieved of the emotion for a moment. Understanding that *this is just mind, and there's no one here, but only conditions* is an insight.

Often, insight minds are momentary and this is normal. We allow these insights to arise repeatedly and gather all these little insights many, many times. The repeated arising of insight impresses that understanding into the mind and each mind that arises then passes along its qualities to the next mind. When insights arise repeatedly, the inheritance of that insight for each successive mind becomes stronger. That's how we get lasting insights.

If you are personally very involved in trying to do the practice, you will not be able to see what is going on naturally.

EFFORTLESS AWARENESS

We always need to remember the difference between personal exertion and the energy of the dhamma taking over. If you are personally very involved in trying to *do* the practice, you will not be able to see what is going on naturally. When you step back you are able to see that the process of awareness is already happening quite naturally. That's why I sometimes ask yogis: Can you notice that you can hear even though you are not listening, that seeing is happening even though you are not trying to look at anything? Can you notice that even though you are not paying attention, your mind already knows things?

I would like yogis, especially for those who have been practicing for years, to get to the point where they realize that without focusing or paying attention, that knowing is happening. After many years of meditating, their practice must have gained momentum and they need to step back in order to see that this is happening. At that point, you need to switch from doing to recognizing. When the dhamma takes over, there is just a doing of what is necessary.

Of course it is not possible to just switch, to immediately change the paradigm. But it is good to have this information because this will enable you to sometimes switch into this new mode. This way you will slowly understand what is actually happening and this will enable you to let go of the old paradigm. That's why momentum is so important, when things continue under their own steam and you can really see that *you* are not involved. If you just practice continuously and correctly, understanding will arise. Once you gain some understanding that this process is just happening, the mind will start seeing things more and more from this perspective.

GATHERING MOMENTUM, COLLECTING GOLD DUST

If you reflect on this life alone and add up the amount of time that you have spent trying to be aware, to grow the practice, and wisdom, you will find that it is a small amount of time. Ignorance and defilements have been our companions from the time we were born. Things may seem impermanent but defilements *always seem to be permanently there!* If you understand cause and effect, however, you'll see that defilements have always had their way. They are the ones whose impressions have run very deep. They are very strongly impressed in the mind and they leave a very long shadow to carry on their work through cause and effect. If our practice is intermittent, then we will not become any more skillful and any understanding will come to a standstill. If we neglect our practice altogether, delusion will begin to grow again and cloud over all the things that we once understood.

So long as we continue meditating, we can maintain a certain level of understanding. Awareness is the ground that allows wisdom to arise over and over again and that's why you have to be aware moment to moment. Any new understandings or wisdom passes away, just like everything else. The understanding of anicca (impermanence) and anatta (not-self, non-ego) are also impermanent. However, while that understanding may arise and also pass away, it will leave an impression for the next mind, which picks it up and in turn leaves an impression as it passes away.

It is a zero sum game: You are either doing *this* or you are doing *that*. If *this* is not present, then *that* is present. You are either moving forward or you are moving backward; there is no standing still. Wholesome minds will support each other just as unwholesome minds support each other. When something is burning and you throw in more water, the fire will go out. If flames are more intense, the fire will continue to burn.

I want you to use your wisdom to continue the work. You collect this gold dust a bit more each day, day by day. You learn from it all while this and that goes on in your lives. Mindfulness is a lifetime commitment, not a part-time job. It is something that you really, really need to do all the time. *All the time.* Only when you see the nature of the mind will you understand the nature of dhamma. The mind is just arising and passing away, is so ephemeral, and the only input you can have to this process is the quality of awareness. When awareness becomes natural, it means that you have been putting in the effort to keep it going: persistence is right effort. Awareness starts staying. Effort remains and it becomes much more natural and much more useful.

Vipassanā wisdom cannot come about through intellectual thinking. It simply cannot be comprehended. Vipassanā insight is not something that can be conceptualized through images; it is a wholly new understanding and insight into principles, into nature.

As we practice diligently and continuously, we will keep having these small understandings and insights over and over. Over the long haul, insights will become so persistent that they will work in tandem with awareness. Once wisdom starts working together with awareness, our meditation moves to a higher level of understanding. We begin to have bigger insights.

These bigger understandings have a life of their own; they have more power. They are not so dependent anymore on awareness. Once we have had such insights, they will always be available and wisdom will always be there. At this stage, awareness will step back to play a secondary role. It will always be present because wisdom cannot exist without awareness, but at this level of understanding, wisdom begins to have a life of its own. Awareness will keep feeding wisdom and our understandings will grow in strength. At this stage, the mind always knows what to do, and it can happen that the practice becomes so easy that it will keep going even if we are not making any effort to practice. The more we practice, the more the mind understands how to practice and it doesn't have to think about how to practice. It finds its way when wisdom starts to operate.

The real benefit of the Dhamma is not to stop engaging with life issues but to approach the same tasks with wisdom instead of defilements, having understood how they work.

May All Beings Be Happy!

Everybody has wholesome and unwholesome qualities in the mind but learning to cultivate the *wholesome qualities* is meditation.

How do we cultivate these good qualities?

Appendix: Mindfulness in Brief

Satipaṭṭhāna, or meditation on the four foundations of mindfulness (body, feelings, mind and dhamma) cultivates the good qualities in our minds. Everybody has wholesome and unwholesome qualities in the mind but learning to cultivate the *wholesome qualities* is meditation. How do we cultivate these good qualities? Meditation involves the things we observe (called *objects*) and that which is observing (the *mind*). It is important to remember that sights, sounds, touch, taste, smells, and thoughts or the experiences arising at the six sense doors do not meditate. We do not have to do anything to these experiences because they will always be there. These objects are just happening in the body and / or mind. Meditation is this latter part, the work of the mind, and the work to transform the mind.

A yogi has three jobs, and we will cover these in turn: 1) to have right view, 2) to be aware, and finally, 3) to practice continuously. When we are experiencing something, we should remind ourselves that it is an object of meditation and that the mind is knowing it. It should not be that *this is a bad experience* or *this is a good experience.* We would like to see things and regard things as they are. What is being known is *just to be known* and not to be loved or hated or desired or pushed away. Instead we remind ourselves that what is happening, what we're experiencing, and what we're observing is all nature. We should remind ourselves that objects will always follow their nature, that they are doing what they are doing, and that they are being seen, heard or experienced. If we don't remind ourselves of this nature, the mind will vacillate, desiring in one moment and resisting in the next moment. Desire and resistance distort the "lenses" of the mind.

While the object itself is not important, we do need to know the object and to see the object clearly. Sometimes I say that we need a 60/40 awareness, which means we pay attention 60% to the observing mind and 40% to the object. We need to pay more attention to the observing mind because defilements like greed, anger, and delusion happen in the mind, and these defilements cover the mind. They prevent us from seeing clearly; we cannot see objects for what they truly are.

Let's look more closely at the different pieces of meditation. There are five qualities in our minds that do the work of meditation. These qualities are awareness, perseverance, faith (or confidence), steadiness or stability of mind, and wisdom. These are the five qualities that we are trying to cultivate in the mind. There are also six sense objects arising at the six sense doors. These six sense objects are our stepping-stones in that we use the objects that arise at the six sense doors to cultivate the five good qualities of the mind.

When we meditate, any phenomenon or experience that is being known becomes an object. We also need to be consciously aware of what we know. We also need to know *how to regard* objects, to have the right view toward the objects, and be able to consider them in the right way. We can do one of these things: we can remember that the objects are just nature, or that the objects are just things that are being known.

In Satipaṭṭhāna, *mindfulness* or *awareness* (as I use the two words interchangeably) is the first of the five wholesome faculties of the mind. We then cultivate the other four faculties through continuous mindfulness. Simply, mindfulness is about remembering to be present in this moment, knowing any one of or all of the six sense objects (mind and/or body) that are happening right now. In English, I like to use words like *awareness*, *mindfulness*, *remembering*, *not forgetting*, *recognizing*, and *noticing* for the Pāḷi word of sati. I prefer not to use terms like *concentrate* or *penetrate into the object* because I don't like the strong sense of effortful energy that is suggested by those words.

I was once sitting in a car driven by a yogi. When another car passed by us the yogi asked, "Is it enough for me to know it as meditation awareness if I knew that a car passed by?" No. It's not quite there yet. We would all know that a car had passed by whether we are meditating or not. How is meditation-knowing different from regular-knowing? There's seeing, hearing, and thinking *and* the meditator knows consciously that these things are being experienced. A non-meditator knows that a car has passed by but does not reference it to his own experience. He may instead refer just to the concept of what has happened where the thought has already processed the whole experience. That is why I say awareness is when you are aware of the six sense objects as your direct experience.

For example, if I am sitting on a rug right now and I'm aware of this rug, this is not considered meditation awareness. When I am aware of *the process of seeing or feeling* that allows me to see and feel and interpret this rug as a rug, this is my experience. I am aware of this experience. Being aware of only the conceptual part of the experience is not sati. We are not as interested in the concept of a rug in-as-much as we are in the process of seeing or feeling. We need concepts in order to function in daily life, but in meditation we want to know the underlying process of what is happening in the mind, of nature, and of reality.

So you are aware and you maintain that awareness. You do not have to use much energy to be aware. There's no need to focus hard but you do need to use right effort to keep reminding yourself to go continuously. If you can use energy in that right way, you can go on practicing the whole day without feeling tired. Try to sustain that awareness for longer periods of time throughout the day.

You can take one object that you know lightly and use that as a grounding object to explore more widely. When I was practicing continuously in daily life, I would use feeling as my touchstone. From there I began to notice how thoughts affected feelings and how feelings affected thoughts. I slowly learned and understood all these relationships.

You can sit, walk, and lie down as you meditate in your daily lives. The posture is not important, and is even less so in daily life where you have to go about your business doing things. The timetable, however, is *all* the time from the moment you wake up in the morning until the moment you fall asleep at night.

You also need to know *how* to view these objects that are arising. Whether they are sense objects or your experience, you need to view them as *nature*. Nature means it is impossible to find a "you" or a "me." Nature is all just a process of cause and effect. There's nothing inherently good or bad in these objects.

If you are developing greed or aversion towards any kind of sound, it indicates that you have a wrong view of the experience.

Come back to the right view when you face difficulties with certain objects: consider sound as just a sound. It is an object and it is just nature. This is the view that you should take. The instruction in the Satipaṭṭhāna Sutta is to *recognize* the experience as it is. If you are developing greed or aversion towards any kind of sound, it indicates that you have a wrong view of the experience. For someone with right view, samādhi, or stability of mind is automatically there.

A concept is just a name given to reality. When you become aware of reality, you can see both the mind that is conceptualizing and reality. You will notice a sound as just a sound (reality) and also an interpretation of the particular sound (concept). When you are crossing the street and you hear a car coming, then you also need to watch out to see if a car is coming. You can know that sound is just sound but wisdom must also understand what that sound means. There are two kinds of wisdom at work here: the wisdom that understands the concept of an approaching car and the wisdom that understands reality of a sound is a sound.

Understanding is different from just experience. Understanding means you get it: This is reality. Sometimes experience does not mean that you *truly understand it* and *the view changes.* You can know that something is an object, which you can't touch or feel but you just understand that this is something that is being known and therefore has the role of being an object.

The same instructions apply for the thinking mind. When you notice that the mind is thinking, know it. If there is less thinking, know that. If there is more thinking, know that. If there is no thinking, know that. Thinking is the mind and the definition of *mind* is that which thinks and that which knows. Problems arise when there is *aversion* to thinking, when you have the idea that you should not be thinking when you are meditating. All sorts of resistance follow that idea. There is no need to struggle with your thoughts because the thinking mind is never a problem. If there is a lot of thinking going on, there is no need to reduce it! All you have to do is acknowledge over and over again that the mind is thinking. After all, you are only able to recognize that amount of thinking because there is awareness!

Yogis label the times when they are lost in thought and don't know that they're thinking because they are lost in thoughts as a *wandering mind*. The mind arises in the present moment and passes away in the present moment. Thoughts about home or work arise in the mind and we can acknowledge these thoughts arising each time it happens. Actually the mind does not wander anywhere nor does it go anywhere; it thinks about the past and future in the present moment.

You can relate to pain in the same way. When you notice even a little bit of pain, first check your attitude. If the mind is feeling uncomfortable, adjust the attitude, remind yourself that this is nature and then, having brought in the right view, watch the discomfort or the aversion in the mind. First, watch the resistance and then you can watch the actual physical sensations. To begin with, why do you observe pain? Do you want to make it go away? It is natural for the body to become uncomfortable if we sit still for long periods. We should observe pain because we want to understand something about the nature of pain; we don't observe pain in hopes that it will go away. Why do you think your leg hurts when it hurts? The simplest answer is that *your leg hurts because you have a leg.* Where there is a body, there will also be physical pain. That is awareness and right view that we can develop.

The final, important piece of a yogi's three jobs is to practice continuously. Whatever you do, first be aware of yourself, and then go about your task. You may have fairly continuous mindfulness when you are sitting in meditation but you will eventually get up. What do you know first when you get up? It could be your hand or legs moving or just the energy you're using to put strength into what you do. Know that and what's happening after that. It's even better when you know all your movements and if you know what is happening in the mind at the same time.

When you do sitting meditation you can take the whole body as an object and know anything that becomes obvious and see it change. If you are used to using an anchor, then use that anchor as a starting point. You can use awareness of breathing in and out at the nostrils (ānāpānasati), rising and falling of the abdomen, or sounds as anchors. These are just a few examples. You can use any object that is easy for you to be aware of as an anchor to establish mindfulness. The anchor just starts the mind off on being mindful and once you are aware of any object for some time, the mind will actually start to know other objects. That is good. It means that mindfulness is getting better. When the mindfulness is good, it begins to feel like it knows four or five objects simultaneously.

You are observing everything to understand the nature of this mind-body experience. What can you understand about these experiences? You have been practicing for a long time, you have been watching the body, watching the mind, and you have been doing it for years. What more have you understood about this body and this mind and the interactions between body and mind?

The goal of Satipaṭṭhāna practice is to understand deeply. When there is right understanding, when we have true realization into the nature of things, there will be calm in the mind. This calm state is a by-product of understanding or insight. The real goal of this meditation is to understand.

How can we understand the nature of pain if we just stared at it and it disappeared? Please be patient. When there is pain, watch the resistance in the mind and do this only for as long as it is bearable. When you change your posture, be aware of two possible motivations behind it: 1) greed to be more comfortable, or 2) understanding that if you continue to sit in that position, your aversion will grow. You don't want to be growing aversion any more than you want to be growing greed. Understanding that the pain might become too much, you let go of the pain and make yourself more comfortable to prevent the growth of aversion.

Finally, let's discuss talking. We should try to practice right speech and only say what is necessary and wholesome and for this we do need mindfulness. Speaking is all around us in daily life. You do not want to cut off speech without awareness of what you need to do. Use some restraint and know, consider and understand before you speak. Then you will also know if there is a need to talk. If you wanted to say something and you refrained from speaking then continue to know and recognize that you are not speaking but see the thinking going on in the mind.

There are many things that can happen while you are talking. If you are triggered when you are talking to someone, the fact that you are triggered but are still there, with the person, might trigger other emotions like embarrassment or agitation. While the mind may still

If you are strongly attached
to ideas, there will be triggers
when someone else presents a
conflicting idea.

be agitated, at the very least, you can still be aware. The purpose of mindfulness of speech is not to have a perfectly wise response, but to have a mindful conversation. You may have lost your balance in that time but what you need to know is that mindfulness is present through it all. If you are strongly attached to ideas, there will be triggers when someone else presents a conflicting idea. It's like North and South Korea being at war, separated by ideology. You can learn some lessons from these conversations when there is mindfulness. Whenever we say something wrong, we will suffer a little bit but if mindfulness stays with us, we will always learn.

Be a little extra careful at home. It is so much more interesting at home when mindfulness is always present, and especially when we bring mindfulness to daily life situations. In your talking to others you learn to see others' intentions and learn to speak in a way that helps you to manage yourself and manage the conversation as well. We begin to know what we are going to say before we say it and eventually have time to choose the skillful path.

Dedication

*This wonderful gift of Dhamma comes to you from the
community of meditators and supporters for whom the Dhamma
has touched in unfathomable ways.*

*May you also reap the benefits of three levels of wisdom
through this Dhamma dana—
in understanding the profound Dhamma,
in practicing rightly the Dhamma and
in reaping the fruit of Dhamma.
And may Nibbāna be the absolute finale.*

Sādhu! Sādhu! Sādhu!